EXPLORING SCOTLAND'S HERITAGE

EXPLORING SCOTLAND'S HERITAGE
GRAMPIAN

Ian A G Shepherd

The Royal Commission
on the Ancient and Historical Monuments
of Scotland

Edinburgh
Her Majesty's Stationery Office

Royal Commission on the Ancient and Historical Monuments of Scotland
54 Melville Street, Edinburgh EH3 7HF (031-225 5994)

The Commission, which was established in 1908, is responsible for compiling a national record of archaeological sites and historic buildings of all types and periods. The Commission makes this record available both through its publications (details of which can be obtained from the above address) and through the maintenance of a central archive of information, known as the National Monuments Record of Scotland, which contains an extensive collection of pictorial and documentary material relating to Scotland's ancient monuments and historic buildings and is open daily for public reference at 6-7 Coates Place, Edinburgh EH3 7AA.

Other titles in the series
Argyll and the Western Isles
Lothian and the Borders
Orkney and Shetland
The Clyde Estuary and Central Region
Dumfries and Galloway
The Highlands
Fife and Tayside

Cover Illustration *Highland Gathering at Balmoral 1869 by Samuel Bough,* courtesy of Aberdeen Art Gallery and Museum

CONTENTS

FOREWORD

Twentieth century Scotland has a heritage of human endeavour stretching back some nine thousand years, and a wide range of man-made monuments survives as proof of that endeavour. The rugged character of much of the Scottish landscape has helped to preserve many antiquities which elsewhere have vanished beneath modern development or intensive deep ploughing, though with some 3,850 km of coastline round mainland alone there has also been an immeasurable loss of archaeological sites as a result of marine erosion. Above all, perhaps, the preservation of such a wide range of monuments should be credited to Scotland's abundant reserves of good building stone, allowing not only the creation of extraordinarily enduring prehistoric houses and tombs but also the development of such remarkable Scottish specialities as the medieval tower-house and the iron-age broch. This volume is one of a series of eight handbooks which have been designed to provide up-to-date and authoritative introductions to the rich archaeological heritage of the various regions of Scotland, highlighting the most interesting and best preserved of the surviving monuments and setting them in their original social context. The time-scale is the widest possible, from relics of World War II or the legacy of 19th century industrial booms back through history and prehistory to the earliest pioneer days of human settlement, but the emphasis varies from region to region, matching the particular directions in which each has developed. Some monuments are still functioning (lighthouses for instance), others are still occupied as homes, and many have been taken into the care of the State or the National Trust for Scotland, but each has been chosen as specially deserving a visit.

Thanks to the recent growth of popular interest in these topics, there is an increasing demand for knowledge to be presented in a readily digestible form and at a moderate price. In sponsoring this series, therefore, the Royal Commission on the Ancient and Historical Monuments of Scotland broadens the range of its publications with the aim of making authentic information about the man-made heritage available to as wide an audience as possible.

The author, Ian A G Shepherd, holds the post of Regional Archaeologist in the Physical Planning Department of Grampian Regional Council, where his involvement in Grampian monuments over the past eleven years has included both surface fieldwork and excavation of sites as widely separated in time as bronze-age burials and Fyvie Castle. He is also familiar with Grampian archaeology from the air, and many of the aerial photographs in this volume are his own work. Since 1982 he has edited the *Proceedings of the Society of Antiquaries of Scotland*.

Monuments have been grouped according to their character and date and, although only the finest, most interesting or best preserved have been described in detail, attention has also been drawn to other sites worth visiting in the vicinity. Each section has its own explanatory introduction, beginning with the most recent monuments and gradually retreating in time back to the earliest traces of prehistoric man.

Each major monument is numbered and identified by its district so that it may easily be located on the end-map, but it is recommended that the visitor should also use the relevant 1:50,000 maps published by the Ordnance Survey as its Landranger Series, particularly for the more remote sites. Sheet nos 27, 28, 29, 30, 36, 37, 38, 43, 44, and 45 cover Grampian Region. The National Grid Reference for each site is provided (eg NJ 684152) as well as local directions at the head of each entry.

An asterisk indicates that the site is subject to restricted hours of opening; unless attributed to Historic Buildings and Monuments, Scottish Development Department (HBM, SDD) or the National Trust for Scotland (NTS), the visitor should assume the monument to be in private ownership and should seek permission locally to view it. It is of course vital that visitors to any monument should observe the country code and take special care to fasten gates. Where a church is locked, it is often possible to obtain the key from the local manse, post office or general store.

We have made an attempt to estimate how accessible each monument may be for disabled visitors, indicated at the head of each entry by a wheelchair logo and a number: 1=easy access for all visitors, including those in wheelchairs; 2=reasonable access for pedestrians but restricted access for wheelchairs; 3= restricted access for all disabled but a good view from the road or parking area; 4=access for the able-bodied only.

Many of the sites mentioned in this handbook are held in trust for the nation by the Secretary of State for Scotland and cared for on his behalf by Historic Buildings and Monuments, Scottish Development Department. Further information about these monuments, including details of guidebooks to individual properties, can be obtained from Historic Buildings and Monuments, PO Box 157, Edinburgh EH3 7QD. Information about properties in the care of the National Trust for Scotland can be obtained from the National Trust for Scotland, 5 Charlotte Square, Edinburgh EH2 4DU. The abbreviation RMS refers to the Royal Museum of Scotland, Queen Street, Edinburgh, whose collections include important material from Grampian.

ANNA RITCHIE
Series Editor

ACKNOWLEDGMENTS

My first thanks are to my wife, Alexandra, not only for her almost unflagging support and encouragement during the preparation of this book, but also for assistance in the final selection of photographs. For her editing skills and patience I am indebted to Dr Anna Ritchie. I am also grateful to my parents, JP and HD Shepherd, for encouraging an early interest in Scottish architecture, both ecclesiastical and castellated, that made the writing of much of this book so pleasurable.

It is also a pleasure to acknowledge the unfailing assistance of the staff of the Royal Commission. I am particularly grateful to the Secretary, Mr JG Dunbar, for reading the typescript and commenting on it so helpfully. I am also indebted to Ian Fleming for checking the grid references and routes, to John Keggie for his excellent interior photographs and to Ian Parker for preparing the maps and plans.

For general advice, information on specific points, or other forms of help, I should like thank Dr DJ Breeze, Dr HAW Burl, Dr DV Clarke, Mr TG Cowie, Dr RA Knox, Mr GS Maxwell, Mr JC Murray, Dr IBM Ralston, Mr M Seton, Mr H Gordon Slade, Mr JA Souter, and Miss AE Woodward.

Finally, I should like to thank Mr TF Sprott, Director of Physical Planning, Grampian Regional Council, and the past chairman of the Planning Property and Development Committee, Councillor E Harrison, for sanctioning my work on the book.

For permission to reproduce photographs I am indebted to the Royal Commission on the Ancient and Historical Monuments of Scotland (Crown Copyright: pp. 19, 24, 31, 34, 35, 37, 38, 40, 41, 54, 67, 75, 76, 77, 79, 80, 82, 95, 100, 102, 109, 110, 112, 130, 145, 155, 158, colour opp. pp. 64, 65, 80, 81, 112, 113); the Royal Museum of Scotland (pp. 13, 14, 15, 99, 120, 133); Historic Buildings and Monuments (Crown Copyright: pp. 86, 108, 111, 123, 176); the Anthropological Museum, University of Aberdeen (p. 141); Aberdeen Art Gallery and Museums (cover); Aberdeen Archaeological Surveys (Crown Copyright: pp. 44, 46, 47, 48, 49, 55, 59, 66, 73, 81, 84, 90, 93, 94, 118, 129, 131, 134, 135, 136, 138, 139, 157). The remainder are the work of the author (copyright Grampian Regional Council).

INTRODUCTION

'Over in the west a long line of lights twinkles against the dark. Whin burning—or the camps of Maglemose?'

The land

By conjuring the image of a band of eight thousand year old hunter-gatherers lying down for their first night in Scotland, 'with their tall, deep-bosomed sinewy mates and their children', from a cluster of fires seen across the Mearns in a Spring twilight, Lewis Grassic Gibbon evokes a central paradox about the area that is now the Grampian Region. Much of this area, comprising the former counties of Aberdeen, Banff, Kincardine and Moray, is rich in history and archaeology; its people have a lively interest in the past and the traveller can in places experience a sense of the great age of human settlement. Yet there are few areas in Scotland whose landscape is so young, so much the product of a single, hectic burst of activity over the last 250 years.

The agricultural improvements of the 18th and 19th centuries (which had their roots in small-scale 17th century experiments in crop rotation and tree planting) wrought such changes on the landscape of Buchan in particular that the 360° panorama from the Hill of Belnagoak, between Methlick and New Deer, shows scarcely a single man-made feature–road dyke, farmhouse, field, even whole towns and villages–that is older than the beginning of last century. And yet the sense of time-depth persists.

Partly this is because, within this 'landscape of improvement', enclaves of the past do survive, whether as tidy National Trust or HBM properties, ribbed hillsides of rig and furrow cultivation, grey prehistoric rings of standing stones or quiet kirkyards. However, a large part of the explanation must relate to the great size of the region itself. Gibbon entitled his essay 'A Land' (although as a good east-coast Scot he was defining Scotland in terms of its agricultural heartland on the east), and it is as a country in more than miniature that we must view the Grampian Region.

Extending to 3500 square miles or 8700 square kilometres (11.3% of the Scottish landmass, see map on back end-paper), it stands in many ways remote from the rest of Scotland. On the way to nowhere but itself, its people quietly, sometimes dourly self-sufficient, it is even furnished with its own southern frontier, the broad estuary of the Esks, although at some periods, during much of prehistory in particular, the real boundary seems to have been to the north, beyond the rich rolling farmland of the Mearns and hard by the hilly ramparts of the Mounth. Four other areas, defined broadly in terms of the evidence for settlement that they contain, lie to north and west of the Mounth: Deeside, the Garioch, Buchan and Moray. These areas are spread out on a series of plateaux at decreasing altitudes, which tilt northwards and eastwards to the sea from the Cairngorm massif in the south-west. A land of open, varied country, with some steeper slopes and massifs rising above the plains and

9

*The landscape of Improvement;
aerial view of Buchan from west of
Methlick*

basins. All these landforms were subject to the effects of the last glaciation, from which the area would have been recovering by c 12,000 BC. The movement of the ice enhanced slopes, deepened river channels and deposited shattered rock, clay, gravel and sand across the area. With the mountains to the west, Grampian is a land of fairly gradual climatic changes: it is also moderately dry. All in all, many parts of this varied landscape have considerable potential for settlement.

The five main sub-areas of the region can be characterized in greater detail (working from south to north). The Mearns, lying south of the steep slopes of the Mounth, is now highly fertile, but in the past its heavy soil would have been difficult to work. This soil, derived from the underlying red sandstone, lies in 'bottom land' locations which would have impeded drainage. Deeside, the catchment area of the major river Dee, has relatively poor land towards its mouth and the enclosing hill-slopes rise quickly to harsher land, but an important area of sheltered gravel slopes occurs on its middle reaches in the Howe of Cromar. The Garioch, in contrast, contains good, well drained soils and comparatively gentle slopes. For our purposes the Garioch will be taken to refer to the fertile heartland of the north-east, embracing the Don and Urie rivers and extending westwards to include the Insch and Rhynie areas. Buchan refers to the great knuckle beyond the Ythan that juts into the North Sea, as well as the Deveron valley west of the high ground between Pennan and New Deer. Moray refers to the land between the great rivers Spey and Findhorn. It contains great variations in landforms, from the light sandy soils of the Laich to the moorland massifs to the south.

Routes into the region are, from the west, along the coastal plain from Inverness, and from the south, through the Mearns and round the high land at Stonehaven. Otherwise more hazardous hill and mountain passes, of which there are 14 over the Mounth, had to be used.

The first inhabitants

Man first reveals himself in Grampian in two unobtrusive, barely perceptible ways. First as handfuls of tiny flint flakes, garnered from the haughs of the Dee and the Ythan and the coastal sand systems of Forvie or Culbin, which represent toolkits for the manufacture of bone fish-spears and other implements of hunting, and second as a few oscillations in the pollen diagram from Braeroddach Loch, Cromar. Yet these meagre data speak of centuries of exploration, hunting, fishing and forest-firing by the hunters and their 'deep-bosomed mates' who had followed the retreating ice northwards more than 8000 years ago. Travelling by the coast and penetrating the north-east along the wooded thickets of the Dee and the Ythan, theirs was a way of life with a certain structure, being based on the cycles of the salmon in the rivers and of the plants and animals in the forest. We must envisage bands of up to four or five families, thoroughly attuned to their environment and capable of manipulating it by forest fires designed to increase the browsing for game, moving regularly over vast forested territories according to the season.

For over 2000 years this way of life endured: its end came gradually, the result of increasing contact with small groups of incomers who possessed the knowledge and skills of farming. From around 4000 BC small family groups with origins ultimately amongst the farming communities of north-west Europe crossed to the east coast of Britain and established themselves in settlements which relied largely on the growing of wheat and barley and the raising of sheep and cattle. The earliest traces of these people are represented by the Balbridie timber hall excavated on Deeside and the series of long cairns and barrows, trapezoidal or oval in plan, that speak of the importance of ancestors to these communities. Such cairns were constructed on skylines within sight of the fields of the community by members of the lineage working as a unit over a considerable time (c 6000

A tomb of ancestors; a skyline long cairn in Deeside

pattern may be interpreted as indicating the colonisation of areas adjacent to the core areas of settlement by groups that came into competition as a result of the shortage of good land in the new areas.

Another type of neolithic burial monument that has a well defined distribution within western Grampian is the Clava cairn. Such cairns have strong links with the recumbent stone circles of Grampian which have traditionally been dated to the second millennium. However, the links between the two types (emphasis on a south-western orientation of major elements, use of quartz, cup-marks, and graded standing stones), their mutually exclusive distributions and the fact that they are both the result of well organised group efforts suggest that they should be viewed as third millennium achievements. Although these rings of stone are now cold and remote from our experience, we should envisage them alive with the flickering of firelight, the gleam of the moon and the insistent drumming of fertility rituals.

Power and prestige

By the middle of the third millennium BC the Garioch had become the main focus for settlement and ritual to the extent that all four of the ceremonial centres known as henges that are recorded in Grampian are to be found in this area. It is possible that they were built or modified in response to a challenge to the supremacy of the area from individuals in Buchan who had acquired a new, high status pottery called beakers. The initial makers of such pottery were metalworkers from the Netherlands who came to eastern Scotland and England. It may be that the old links between the Deveron basin and Ireland, seen in neolithic pottery from Auchterless and Old Deer and in the origin of the recumbent stone circles and the stone-axe trade, were revived at this time for the import of Irish copper. Certainly the concentration of stone moulds on the Deveron indicates early

man-hours in the case of the Dalladies mound in the Mearns), stressing the importance of the group as opposed to the individual. Conflicts within the group could therefore be resolved by appeal, through rituals invoking the mystery of death conducted at the tomb, to the common ancestors who were still present at the heart of the community.

From the distribution of neolithic pottery and polished stone axes the core areas of settlement in Grampian in the fourth millennium can be inferred to be the Garioch and the Laich of Moray. However, the two dozen or so long cairns and barrows in Grampian show an interesting absence from these core areas (barring three simple examples) and instead cluster in the Mearns, east Buchan, and the lower Deveron where several complex monuments are found. This

metalworking. Whatever the mechanism, the new, seemingly magical skills of metalworking and the change in burial rite to inhumation of individuals in single short cists both represented a means for individuals to acquire and demonstrate status independent of the traditional, group-dominated ways.

It is striking that the earliest beakers (with two exceptions) avoid the traditional power centres of the Laich and the Garioch. However, it is only in Buchan that a complete sequence of beaker pottery can be traced, while it is also no accident that the earliest type of metal dagger was found in Auchterless. Such evidence suggests that certain individuals in Buchan rapidly acquired the means of controlling the

manufacture and distribution of prestige goods. The Garioch was not to catch up for several generations: eventually a large number of local copies of late Dutch metalworkers' beakers were made and deposited in cists. The manner in which beakers are found on sites representative of the earlier social order suggests, if not a deliberate slighting of the power and authority that they represent, at least the establishment of a new ritual benchmark, a point of change. For example, fragments of four beakers were placed in the neolithic burial mound at Pitglassie, Auchterless, a complete beaker and fragments of two others were placed in a pit beside the similar mound at Boghead, Fochabers and one was deposited in a pit as the final traceable act at the Berrybrae stone circle. An important, if enigmatic, type of ceremonial object which was well represented in Grampian at this time is the carved stone ball. Sometimes enhanced with intricate symbols, the possession of such balls as that from Towie may have conferred particular power or prestige on an individual.

Bronze technology developed during the second millennium and its products spread unevenly throughout the north-east: there are interesting gaps in Cromar and the Mearns. It is clear that bronze axes and halberds in particular were used in competitive or boundary situations: the eight flat axes from beneath a stone at Finglenny, Rhynie, three of which had been snapped in half, are an example of ostentatious disposal of wealth, while the pair of axes found high on a scree at Ballater may mark in a ritual manner the limit of settlement on Deeside at the time.

Many of the 600 or so round burial cairns belong to this period. Some, such as those south of Keith or in Strathdon may indicate expansion of settlement into poorer land. Other ritual monuments show a marked reduction in size during the second millennium; for example, late stone circles such as Glassel or Templestone, and kerb cairns, often clustered close together as at Forvie.

A symbol of prestige: carved stone ball from Towie, Strathdon

13

Defence and display: Celts and Picts

From around 1200 BC the archaeological record in Grampian changes in a way that reflects, at a distance, the profound changes that were taking place in southern Britain and across Europe at this time. Although the climate was gradually deteriorating, agriculture was pursued tenaciously in certain more favoured areas. This is illustrated by the 1000 year-long phase of continuous woodland clearance and cultivation seen in the pollen diagram from Braeroddach Loch, Cromar. From c 1200 BC the slopes around the loch were being determinedly stripped and ploughed by farmers intent on planting barley. So enthusiastic was the cultivation that a greatly increased volume of sediment built up in the loch, representing bare topsoil that had been washed downslope into the loch. It is no coincidence that one of the largest

The disposal of wealth: a hoard of flat bronze axes from Finglenny, Rhynie

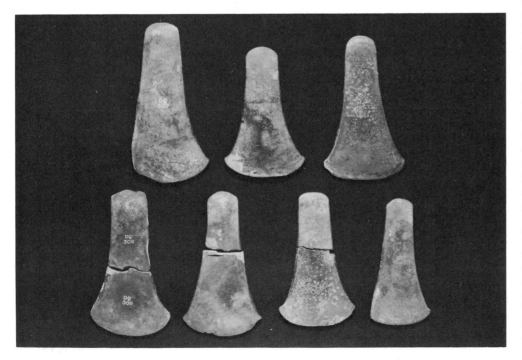

systems of stone clearance heaps to be found in Grampian lies on the hill above Braeroddach.

The onset of wetter weather would have increased pressure on those areas with lighter, well-drained soils and slopes with good run off. The social stress that would have been engendered is indicated by the series of metalwork hoards deposited in watery contexts, particularly peat bogs, between the eighth and sixth centuries BC. The occurrence in such hoards of objects current in north Germany is important in indicating a contact between north-east Scotland and a Europe that was becoming increasingly controlled by a hierarchy of warriors and warlords. The recovery of two bronze parade shields from a moss at Auchmaleddie, New Deer is a good illustration of this warlike influence (translated into a votive deposit), as are the local copies of continental bronze swords from Tarves and other easterly locations. Whether these objects can be interpreted as evidence of actual incursions of continental warriors has been doubted in recent years. However, other evidence, such as the more mundane chisel found in the metal-working area of the Castle Point promontory fort (no. 73), the timber and stone wall of north European inspiration at the same fort, or the human head cult and armlets found in late bronze-age levels in the Sculptor's Cave, Covesea, suggests that at least some members of the north European Celtic-speaking tribes entered the north-east during the first millennium BC. In them we can see the foundations of the hierarchical society that was to exist with little change for the next 1500 years.

The adoption of iron technology, evidence for which appears c 500 BC, might initially have been a destabilizing influence in terms of its impact on existing networks of production and exchange. Control of the new processes intensified competition between different tribes and communities. Increased tensions show in the six types of defended settlement that developed in Grampian during the first

One of a pair of bronze parade-shields deposited in a moss at Auchmaliddie, New Deer, c 700 BC

Snake armlet, cast in bronze, from the Culbin Sands, Moray

millennium BC, which are impressive in their diversity, both in location and size. They range from the 21 hectares of the enclosure at 500 m OD on Tap o'Noth (no. 78) to the c 0.1 ha of the coastal promontory fort of Green Castle, Portknockie, at an elevation of 25 m. For some communities, the need for defence was limited to simple stockaded enclosures; for others, single circuits of rampart and ditch or small stone-walled affairs would suffice. In the main, these forts are subdued features, capping moderate hills. For some communities, however, the aggressiveness of their (?immigrant) neighbours or the dictates of inter-group rivalry led them to create more elaborate defensive structures, such as the three ranks of banks and ditches and the pair of (later) stone walls that crown the Barmekin of Echt (in whose lea Gibbon completed *Grey Granite* shortly before he died).

Perhaps the most dramatic forts are those whose walls were built higher and narrower as a result of baulks of

timber set longitudinally and transversely in the core. The great grey, blank walls that crowned conspicuous heights such as Dunnideer (no. 75), Tap o'Noth or Doune of Relugas were proud assertions of their builders' power and wealth. What we see today at these sites, tumbled blocks of fused stone or screes of slag-like rubble, tell of the wreaking of a terrible, if long-postponed, vengeance on such seemingly invulnerable assertions of power. The timber-lacing in the walls allowed successful attackers to fire the wall, after much labour in piling brushwood against it, in order to collapse it. This may have been as much a psychological as a practical gesture: Tap o'Noth, in particular, would have burned for days, its flaming defeat visible to all inhabitants of the Garioch.

By the end of the millennium, there are indications that the population increased and that farming gradually became more controlled. The concentration of underground storehouses or souterrains in upper

15

Donside and Cromar speaks of control of production and distribution of agricultural and dairy produce. The distribution of fine metalwork (horsegear, weaponry, armlets—aristocratic trappings) coincides well with such evidence for intensification of farming, particularly on the Rhynie/Aboyne axis. There is also a concentration on the Culbin Sands, related to the good soils of the Laich and to the forts there and on the Findhorn.

The society implied by such fine metalwork as the war trumpet from Deskford, the chariot burial from Ballindalloch or the citadel of Tap o'Noth was a warrior aristocracy little different from the barbarian Celtic tribes on the continent. Indeed, Tacitus records that the Caledonii whom the Romans encountered were no different from the rest of the Britons or Gauls in language, religion and rituals. It is important to realise that, as far as the north-east is concerned, the Romans made little impact. Two campaigns (c AD 84 and early third century) have left the name of the north-east tribe (*Taezali*), the ditches of the legions' marching camps, a few artefacts and an as yet unlocated battle, *Mons Graupius*, a 'propaganda victory' (perhaps near Bennachie), in which the tribesmen were defeated but which was not consolidated by the Romans.

Apart from these interruptions (and the possible indirect effect of more substantial Roman activity in the south which may have brought displaced natives to the north-east), the tribal society of the early and middle first millennium AD that we know as Pictish was a development from the preceding millennium. It was structured under potentates, kings, sub-kings, and chiefs, whose culture was of ultimately Celtic origin, as exemplified by the names of their earliest warriors, *Calgacus*, 'the Swordsman', *Argentocoxos*, 'Silver Leg'. The main evidence for the Picts in Grampian is the wealth of early representations of art of sub-Roman iron-age inspiration consisting of animal and object symbols incised on freestanding boulders and slabs which may have functioned as burial markers, the existence of placenames beginning with *pit* (indicating a portion of land), some portable objects of high status and several defended sites, principally the formidable fortress of Burghead.

From the beginning of the 9th century the violent incursions of the Vikings were besetting Pictland to the north, west and south, and even possibly affecting the north-east directly: the timber-laced wall at Green Castle, Portknockie is late enough to have been built against the Norse. By the late 10th or early 11th centuries the tribal Pictish kingdoms in the north-east had been transformed under Scottish kings from Dalriada in Argyll, who had been ruling the adjacent kingdoms of the Picts and Scots jointly since the late 8th century, into areas administered by 'governors' and *mormaers*, the latter possibly from the families of the former potentates.

Pictish symbol stone at Broomend of Crichie (no. 87)

Feudalism

During the 11th century the structure of a fully medieval society developed under the Canmore dynasty of Scottish kings. The two succeeding centuries saw rapid changes in the church, military architecture and in the development of trading settlements. These came about largely through the adoption of Norman practices in a conscious attempt to extend royal authority. In the north-east some of the existing magnates and several members of Anglo-Norman families from the south were granted areas of land, baronies or knight's fees (or feus) in return for military service under the king. The origin of many famous north-east families, eg the Bissets, Burnetts and Irvines, can be seen in this process. In turn these magnates could grant smaller parcels of land to their relations and followers, thereby creating a centralised system of authority, obligations for services and rents.

The Bass of Inverurie, a symbol of feudal power

The military basis of this system would have been emphasised by the raw strength of the newly formed mottes or castle mounds from which the barons would have governed. On a misty day at Duffus (no. 32) or Inverurie, it is still possible to imagine the starkness of the steep-sided mound of beaten earth and turf that had been torn from the boggy surroundings and capped with a strong timber tower. By the early 14th century several notable stone castles had been established, such as the mighty tower of Drum (no. 31) and the grim enclosures of Kildrummy (no. 30), Coull, Balvenie (no. 29) and Fyvie (no. 23).

Significant changes also occurred in the Church, which, after a beginning that is still imperfectly understood (prior to 1131 there was a bishop's seat at Mortlach and very early foundations at Turriff and Aberdour), positively mushroomed buildings and new communities. The bishoprics of Aberdeen and Moray were founded in the 1130s when the Scottish diocesan and parochial structure was reorganised. The earliest extant church in Grampian is the serene little kirk of Birnie (no. 57), dating from 1140. Of the other 12th century foundations the abbey at Kinloss (1159) is largely and the priory of Urquhart (1125) totally destroyed, while the simple chancel of the priory church of Monymusk (no. 55) (1170) remains. There was a concentrated bout of parish church building during the 13th century of which those at Auchindoir (no. 54), Arbuthnott (no. 53), Altyre and Mortlach (no. 56) survive. The abbeys of Deer and Pluscarden (no. 46) were also founded. However, the most important and beautiful medieval building in Grampian was Elgin Cathedral (no. 47, 1224, rebuilt 1270), an expression at once of the wealth, piety and architectural sophistication of the bishopric of Moray.

The wealth necessary for such a building would have come partly from revenues from land granted to the cathedral by the king and other rich barons, but also from a newly expanding class, the burgesses of the newly founded trading burghs. Aberdeen, Banff, Cullen, Elgin, Forres and possibly Kincardine had become royal centres by the end of the 12th century. Such royal burghs were granted rights to conduct markets (and from 1364 to engage in foreign trade): justice was also administered in courts held within the burgh by the king's own officers, the sheriffs.

This apparently well-ordered system was fractured by the Wars of Independence (1296–1336) of which Grampian felt the first, brutal phases worst. In 1296 Edward I of England occupied Elgin, Aberdeen, Banff, Fyvie, Lumphanan and Dunnottar. In the first decade of the 14th century Bruce crushed the Comyn earls of Buchan in the battles of Slioch, Barra and Aiky Brae, part of the 'harrying of Buchan', while in 1336 Edward III burned (Old) Aberdeen. In the previous year, the battle of Culblean, in Cromar, had been an important victory for the Guardian of Scotland, Sir Andrew Moray.

The struggles between king and baron that occupied the end of the 14th and the beginning of the 15th century are marked by the continuing development of castles, as represented by those at Duffus, Darnaway and Dunnottar, and by the iconoclasm of Alexander Stewart, Earl of Buchan and 'Wolf of Badenoch' in burning Elgin Cathedral (and the burghs of Forres and Elgin) in 1390. The massive yet sophisticated mid 15th century palace of the Bishops of Moray at Spynie was no more than necessary. Elgin also suffered in 1402 in a raid by Alexander of the Isles. The threat to the douce traders and farmers of the lowland north-east from 'Highland caterans' is a theme that continues almost to the present: it was perhaps seen most dramatically at the battle of Harlaw (1411), near Inverurie where Donald of the Isles was defeated by the earl of Mar and sundry burgesses of Aberdeen, which stout burgesses are commemorated in a singular memorial erected on the site 500 years later by their successors in burghal office.

Renaissance

The later 15th and early 16th century saw the north-east making considerable intellectual contributions to Scottish life, particularly through the foundation of the university in 1494 (originally called St Mary's, later King's College) and the publication of the *Aberdeen Breviary* (1510), Bishop Elphinstone's Scots Catholic liturgy. The great heraldic ceiling of St Machar's (1520) is a firm statement of Scotland's role in Catholic Europe. Greater emphasis on personal salvation led to the foundation of collegiate churches for the saying of masses for the souls of the dead: the reconstruction of Cullen church in 1543 as a chantry for Alexander Ogilvie of that ilk is a particularly good example of this change.

However, a more radical change came in 1560 with the Reformation. Although it was not pursued as fanatically as in other parts of Scotland, it still had an immediate impact in the north-east, the choir of St Machar's being demolished in 1560 and the lead being stripped off Elgin in 1568. Another result of the Reformation might be said to be the foundation, in 1593, of the second university in Aberdeen by the Earl Marischal, Lord Keith, as a purely Protestant establishment in distinction to the traditionalist King's.

The later 16th century was inevitably a period of division in which religious differences were compounded by endemic family rivalries. In 1562 Mary Queen of Scots was compelled to campaign against the Catholic Gordon earl of Huntly whom she defeated at the battle of Corrichie on the slopes of the Hill of Fare. An indication of the scope for feuds both within and between families can be gauged from the fact that by the end of the 16th century two-thirds of some 600 land-owning families in Aberdeenshire shared just 12 surnames: ie Gordons, Hays, Burnets, Bissets, Frasers, Forbes, Leiths, Keiths, Leslies, Ogilvies, Farquharsons and Irvines. The enmity between the Catholic Gordons and the Protestant Forbeses spilled

The ruins of Elgin Cathedral (William Clark, 1826)

refurbishment was heralded at Huntly by the Z-plan Gordon 'palace' of c 1550 and the later (1606) oriels and heraldic doorway and by the completion of the Forbes range at Tolquhon in 1584. The most consummate work includes Crathes (1596), the Seton work at Fyvie (c 1600) and, the most sublime, Craigievar (1626). And yet, amidst this high flowering of the Scots renaissance in the north-east the life of the lesser folk was still uncertain, if not unspeakably cruel, as the burning of nearly 20 so-called 'witches' by 'triumphant Calvinists' in Aberdeen in 1597 testifies.

In many respects this catalogue of opposites continued throughout the 17th century in the north-east as a result of the religious divisions centering on the Civil War and Covenanters. Aberdeen was mercilessly sacked in 1644 by the highlanders of the Marquess of Montrose, and Dunnottar was beseiged and Brodie Castle burned in 1645, yet in general the north-east again proved unwilling to endorse wholeheartedly savage religious intolerance, although the treatment of those imprisoned in Dunnottar in 1685 can scarcely be described as gentle. However, the attempts in the middle of the century by the 'Aberdeen Doctors' to preserve the unity of a moderate Protestant reformation mirror in some respects the European perspective of the late medieval Aberdeen bishops such as Dunbar and Elphinstone.

over into real violence, as at the battle of Tillyangus (1571), the burning of Corgarff Castle and its inhabitants (immortalised in *Edom o'Gordon*) as well as in the rout of the Crabstane (1571). It is little wonder that both the Frasers and the Forbeses have a tradition that 20 Gordons were done to death while enjoying their hospitality at either Muchalls (Castle Fraser) or Druminnor. It has been rightly said (and by a Gordon) that this story reflects 'the fact that many people thought that there were at least 20 Gordons who would be the better for the letting of a little life out of them'.

By the end of the 16th century such rivalries were becoming increasingly translated into more pacific pursuits such as architectural patronage. The great period of tower-house construction and castle

Cullen old kirk, adapted by lairds and presbyteries over the centuries

The Age of Improvement

The roots of many of the changes which took place in the classic period of agricultural and economic improvement in the 18th and 19th centuries can be found in the 17th century. For example, the quarrying and burning of lime for fertiliser began in the 17th century near Strichen and in Strathisla, while some experiments with crop rotation, including the introduction of peas, also had 17th century beginnings. Tree planting to remedy centuries of felling that had laid much of the north-east landscape bare and windswept began at Brodie in 1650.

In spite of some problems caused by such Jacobite diversions as the landing of the Old Pretender at Peterhead and his proclamation at the Mercat Cross in Aberdeen, the 18th century did see great improvements. The principal instigators of change were landowners like Sir Archibald Grant of Monymusk, Barclay of Urie and James Anderson of Udny who granted 'improving leases' to selected tenants. Under these leases the small, medieval multiple tenancies based on an infield/outfield/pasture system in which a limited range of crops, principally oats, was cultivated on stony, high-backed rigs by teams of oxen held in common was to be replaced by longer, more varied crop rotations in larger, enclosed fields. Such methods increased agricultural production markedly, but also displaced many former tenants.

In order to provide markets for the increased produce and also to redeploy some of the displaced labour, a considerable number of new settlements or planned villages were established throughout the north-east, principally between 1750 (New Keith) and 1825 (Lumsden). (Several new fishing villages had already been established on the north coast in the early years of the century: they were to be followed by others, eg Burghead, a century later.) As with the farming improvements, the initiative generally came from landowners with the capital, the enterprise and the vision. This latter quality was sometimes over-inflated,

as James Boswell noted on his visit to Laurencekirk in 1773:

'Lord Gardenston is the proprietor . . . and has encouraged the building of a manufacturing village, of which he is exceedingly fond, and has written a pamphlet upon it, as if he had founded Thebes . . .'

Laurencekirk was described as a 'manufacturing village' and it is clear that many of the tenants of these new villages were expected to practise cottage industries such as spinning and weaving. Newspaper advertisements of 1772 encouraged weavers to settle in New Byth with guarantees of '. . . the work in their own homes, and that for twelve month certain'. However, planned villages in Grampian remained largely agricultural in nature as craft workers were drawn off to the emerging industrial centre of Aberdeen to work in, for example, paper mills (Peterculter mill opened 1751; Stoneywood 1771) or to woollen mills in Elgin and Keith. (Flax milling also came early to the north-east, the first one in Scotland being opened in Inverbervie in 1788.)

Landowners also initiated major tree-planting schemes at, for example, Monymusk estate (where 50 million trees are claimed) and at Haddo.

Such improving landowners and other 'heritors' in a parish also provided money for new church building, in particular during the middle decades of the 18th century. This was partly because the existing churches were by now in very poor condition and largely in response to the demands of the rigorous Presbyterian liturgy, which emphasised the preaching of the word, that had been finally accepted by the last decade of the 17th century in the 'church by law established'. It may be said that this settlement was not without hardship to many north-east ministers of Episcopalian bent. This is the period of the characteristic plain rectangular or T-plan kirk, the word being preached from imposing pulpits set in the centre of the congregation, as at Dyke, with its grandiose three-decker of 1781. The continuing influence of the lairds

Monymusk village

can be seen in many kirks, most engagingly in the memorials at Monymusk and most remarkably in the laird's loft and stained glass of Fyvie. This established church was riven in 1843 by the Disruption in which almost one third of clergy and congregations left, on the issue of heritors' influence, to form the Free Church. Their return, barring some rumps, in 1929 has produced a legacy of many 19th century buildings now redundant. Some were architecturally distinguished, such as Trinity Alvah, Banff.

By the end of the 18th century communications at last began to improve. Several important stone, and later, iron, bridges were built and from 1800 began to become part of the system of improved turnpike roads. Great improvements were also made to the harbours of the region, beginning with the building of Peterhead's in 1773. Lighthouses were constructed, the earliest in Scotland to be lit being that on Kinnaird Head in Fraserburgh, in 1787 (no. 16). In 1820 the clipper, the *Tourist*, started plying between Aberdeen and Leith, slashing the journey time to the south.

The importance of Aberdeen as an import/export point was considerably increased in 1805 by the opening of the Aberdeenshire canal which ran to Port Elphinstone, beside Inverurie. This permitted fertiliser, agricultural implements and tile drains to be carried into the centre of the Garioch to fuel the continuing agricultural improvements and also allowed the export of the produce of the area, such as grain, meal, stone, slates. Grampian's canal age was to be short, however, for in 1850 the canal was bought by the Aberdeen Huntly railway company who used much of its bed for their line. This new age developed rapidly and by 1865 twenty-two other lines had been established, which, with the turnpikes, formed at long last an efficient communications system for the north-east.

Many industries flourished during the 19th century, including those mentioned above whose origins were in the 18th century: the huge water wheel from the Grandholm woollen mill now in the Royal Museum of Scotland is an example of the scale of this industry. Granite quarries became increasingly numerous: the

Bon Accord Crescent, Aberdeen

first major example was at Cairngall, Longside (1808): the mechanisation of 1834 allowed the industry to expand into world markets. The Foudland slate quarries also flourished. After the Act against small distilleries of 1814, the licensing that began in 1823 led to the industry we see today.

Agricultural improvement continued with unrelenting toil, aided from the 1840s by underground tile drainage and improved ploughs. Between 1814 and 1840, 2000 acres of 'waste' on the Dunecht estates were reclaimed, while between 1807 and 1877 the tilled area of Kincardine increased by 70%. Improving tenancies would be taken even on the most unpromising land. A tide line of impoverished crofts can be seen on Bennachie, on the Buchan mosses (eg encircling Middlemuir Moss) and on upper Deeside.

By the end of the 19th century much of the landscape of the north-east that we see today had been formed, barring the particular contribution of modern forestry. The townscapes had also been transformed, none more so than Aberdeen's which benefited from three fine architects, Archibald Simpson and John Smith in the early 19th century and, subsequently, Marshall Mackenzie who with grace, boldness and flair rose to the challenge of building in that most intractable but beautiful of materials, granite. Buildings of classical inspiration such as the Music Hall (1822), the Clydesdale Bank (1839/42) or the layout of the townscape around Bon Accord Square show Simpson working at his graceful best, while Smith's screen for St Nicholas's kirkyard is cool and precise. Mackenzie's Art Gallery, War Memorial, and Marischal College are confident, poised and capricious in turn.

No account of the recent history of the north-east would be complete without an acknowledgment of the role that the area, Deeside in particular, occupies in popular imagination as a result of its association with the Royal Family. Barring George IV's short but extravagant visit to Edinburgh in 1822, no British monarch between Charles II and Queen Victoria visited Scotland. The purchase, therefore, in 1852 of the Balmoral estate by Prince Albert stimulated considerable interest in the north-east, while the building of William Smith's Balmoral Castle (1855) showed the royal couple to be major supporters of a comparatively restrained version of the Scots Baronial style. This, and the Queen's evident pleasure in local history and landscape and in the naturalness and dignity of the inhabitants, fuelled the taste for the romantic that was already developing throughout Britain. That this taste extended to the hosting of such Highland Gatherings as the one portrayed on the cover of this book (with an origin in societies like the Lonach, founded 1822), which run counter to the lowland north-east Scot's distaste of most things Highland, is but one more delightful paradox of this most diverse region.

1

THREE BURGHS

The burghs of Grampian contain a wide range of interesting townscapes which reflect their varied origins. The three burghs selected for more extensive description were all important royal centres by AD 1200. The trading rights and privileges granted by the king to the burgesses of these and other early burghs, such as Forres, whose medieval layout is still remarkably well-preserved, gave the towns the opportunity to grow and prosper.

Growth was not, however, an inevitable result of the granting of burgh status. The royal burgh of Kintore, for example, which was founded in the late 12th century and received a new charter in 1506, did not

Castle Street, Aberdeen on a market day c 1920

Kintore: the town house of 1734

expand markedly, although its notable town house of 1734 belies this fact.

Other burghs did grow, only to fail subsequently as a result of physical or administrative changes. The burghs of Spynie, north of Elgin, and Rattray, north of Peterhead, both died after the inlets of the sea on which they stood silted up. (The lochs of Spynie and Rattray remain.) The growth of Stonehaven at the expense of the old royal centre of Kincardine is an example of more complex forces, including its proximity to the Earl Marischal's fortress of Dunnottar, its central position in the county of Kincardine, and its charter of 1587. All that remains of Kincardine are the very ruinous castle (NO 671751) and the mercat cross, removed to Fettercairn (NO 650735) around 1730.

Trade with continental Europe in later medieval and renaissance times was of great importance to several north-east ports, principally Aberdeen, but including Elgin (through Spynie), Portsoy, Banff and Peterhead.

In later centuries, a wide variety of needs and activities led to the growth of towns and villages. The wholesale planning of completely new settlements during the 18th and 19th centuries is outlined in the next chapter. These were often intended to foster rural industries such as weaving. The fishing communities also expanded greatly, a result of the increased catching power of the boats and the access to wider markets

The mercat cross of Kincardine, once a royal centre (now in Fettercairn)

Castle Street, Aberdeen: the Town House, the Tolbooth and part of the Clydesdale Bank

that came from improved communications. Fraserburgh, Peterhead, Macduff and Gardenstown all flourished during the 19th century. Certain inland burghs, such as Turriff and Huntly, developed into thriving market and service centres for the improved farms around, while Inverurie owed its 19th century prosperity first to the Aberdeenshire Canal, and then to the railway works. Yet other towns developed as early tourist centres, for example the upland spa of Ballater or the bracing marine resort of Lossiemouth.

The three burghs described next all have a rich legacy of buildings which reflect many of these developments.

Aberdeen Harbour, Provost Ross's House and the towers of the Town House and Marischal College

Aberdeen

NJ 9406.

'.... Whether due to an early manifestation in the founders of the city of that shrewdness and vision which characterise their descendants to this day, or to the necessity of early communal efforts for self-preservation, there appears little doubt that in early times Aberdeen was a town of substantial importance, long before the Capital had attained any considerable civic significance, and while the great City of the Clyde was still a mean cluster of hovels round the palace of the bishop'.

The Freedom Lands and Marches
of Aberdeen 1319-1929 (1929).

Although modern scholarship might not support every detail of this engaging piece of civic pride, the world view implicit in it did much to shape the Aberdeen we see today. Medieval Aberdeen was, in fact, a jumble of timber and wattle houses, hovels, yards and middens perched on three small sand and gravel hills (Castlehill, Gallowgate Hill and St Katharine's Hill) with small lochans and other mounds around. The castle lay to the east, the city kirk, St Nicholas's, outside the gates to the west, a large loch to the north (commemorated in Loch Street) and the Dee estuary to the south.

The present townscape is the result of the *Aberdeen New Streets Act* of 1800 which inaugurated a hectic half century of civil engineering and construction. During this time Aberdeen's population more than doubled, owing to the influx of workers displaced by the agricultural improvements seeking work in the new textile mills or weaving shops of the city. Huge town planning changes were implemented, the most dramatic being the creation of Union Street in 1801 (named after the union of the British and Irish Parliaments that year), which involved the removal of St Katharine's Hill at the west end of the Castlegate and the erection of a series of great arches and viaducts stretching for 0.85 km from Adelphi to Diamond Street. The scheme was conceived by Charles

Abercrombie, a turnpike engineer. Its impact on the town was at first debilitating, for from 1817 to 1825 the burgh could not meet the interest charges on the huge loans raised to finance the work; the city was rescued by the boom in trade.

A walk through the centre of Aberdeen should begin in Castle Street, originally the Castlegate, at the east end of Union Street. Here, on a hill above the mouth of the Dee the 13th century royal castle stood; the site lies behind the baronial pastiche of the Salvation Army citadel (1896) to the east and is now built over. (A fragment of the Cromwellian bastion survives.)

The sandstone mercat cross, the finest in Scotland, was the work of John Montgomery of Old Rayne in 1686. It is circular, with tall arcading surmounted by a unique sequence of portrait medallions of ten Stewart sovereigns, starting with James I on the north-west and a series of fierce gargoyles. The cross shaft, with its white marble unicorn finial, rises above.

Here, at the heart of the old burgh, the traveller is surrounded by grey granite—gleaming, dull, uncompromising, sparkling, unreal by turn, according to the light—all wrought in the 19th century from the city quarries of Loanhead, Dancing Cairns, Sclattie and, principally, Rubislaw.

From the mercat cross, the triumphant corner work, the Clydesdale Bank (formerly the North of Scotland Bank) can be appreciated. Built between 1839 and 1842 by Archibald Simpson, the ninth son of an Aberdeen burgess, its bold Corinthian portico set on the curve carries the building brilliantly round the corner into King Street. Above, the terracotta sculpture group of Ceres, goddess of plenty, by James Giles, is a colourful surprise. The excellent plasterwork of the banking hall includes a gilded version of the Parthenon frieze. This is seen as the climax of Simpson's work. Simpson's other major building in this area is the Atheneum or Union Buildings of 1818-22, whose strong east end faces the cross and the little well-head figure known as the Mannie.

Opposite the Atheneum, on the north side of the street, is the Town House, a bold and successful four-storey granite ashlar building in 'Flemish medieval' style by Peddie and Kinnear, 1868-74. Built as municipal offices and courthouse, its arcaded ground floor, with dwarf gallery above and the projecting 'tourelles'—semi-round towers—complemented by the great corner belfry tower, make a strong and utterly distinctive building, redolent of Victorian burghal prosperity. The metal sundial of 1730 on the corner comes from the old town house, of which the substantial Tolbooth of 1615 survives on the east end of the present building. Its fine lead spire on the bartizaned clock tower still rises from Lodge Walk, the arched pend.

The walker is already approaching the western limits of medieval Aberdeen. To view the southern parts he should descend the Shiprow (from Exchequer Row where the mint was in the 12th century). Provost Ross's house stands halfway down the brae with a view over the harbour. This fine town mansion of 1593 consists of a rectangular main block and two gabled towers. It is now the City's excellent Maritime Museum. The house takes its name from Provost John Ross of Arnage, who traded with the Low Countries in the late 17th century.

At the bottom of Shiprow, turn left to 35 Regent's Quay. Originally a mansion of 1770, this elegant three-storeyed ashlar building became the Customs House. The doorpiece is a pedimented surround by James Gibbs. Aberdeen's harbour developed through the burgh's continental trade; there is a good account of its history in the Maritime Museum.

Returning to the Castlegate by way of Marischal Street provides an opportunity to view one of the pronounced hills, the Castlehill, on which medieval

Aberdeen developed and to appreciate the radical solution to the development of the town to the west and south represented by the construction in 1800 of the viaducts that support Marischal and Union Streets. (The bridge over Virginia Street is a modern replacement.)

Opposite the top of Marischal Street is King Street, the entire south end of which, from Castle Street to Queen Street, forms 'an imposing sequence of integrated classical design', largely the work of Archibald Simpson and the city architect John Smith (appointed 1804). The Medical Hall, no. 29, of 1818/20, is Simpson's first important design in granite. It has a massive Greek Revival Ionic portico and is flanked by two buildings by Smith, built in 1832/3 which were

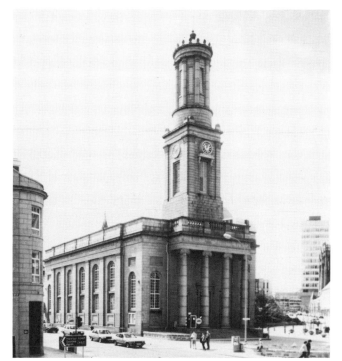

Aberdeen: the North Kirk

deliberately set back to enhance and balance Simpson's strong portico.

Opposite is one of the few sandstone buildings in this part of Aberdeen, St Andrew's Episcopal Cathedral, built in stone from Edinburgh's Craigleith quarry for reasons of cost. In a 'neo perpendicular' style by Archibald Simpson in 1816/17, the high bright chancel was added in 1880 by G E Street and the porch, by Sir Robert Lorimer, in 1911. However, the church owes its present beauty largely to the refurbishing by Sir Ninian Comper between 1936 and 1943. It is difficult to fault Sir John Betjeman's description of St Andrew's as 'Aberdeen's best modern building. . . . You push open the door and your heart gives a leap—there, stretching away as in an old Dutch oil painting is Comper's superb renovation of the interior'. There are two important memorials, one a statue of Bishop John Skinner (whose father's grave is at Longside, no. 36), the other the Seabury memorial which commemorates the consecration, in 1784, of Samuel Seabury as Bishop of Connecticut and hence the first Episcopalian bishop in North America. Comper's restoration was gifted by the American Episcopal church, hence the arms of the states of the American Union on the aisle vaulting.

The east side of the street preserves the original round-headed windows to the ground floors. At the corner of King Street and West North Street is one of John Smith's finest creations, the North Church of 1829-30, now the Arts Centre. Continuing the Greek Revival theme of this town-scape, it is a strong rectangular building with a giant, four column Ionic portico above which soars a splendid square tower with 'Tower of Winds' top stage.

A full left turn into Queen Street and then a right turn at Greyfriars Church (1903, on old site) brings the walker into Broad Street beneath the 'soaring, surging verticals' of Marshall Mackenzie's 'Tudor Gothic' facade of Marischal College (completed 1906). In this

Marischal College: Mackenzie's exuberant facade

Across Broad Street from Marischal, in the shadow of a monstrous civic tower block, is Provost Skene's House, a rare survival of a fine late 16th century town house. Named after Sir George Skene, Provost of Aberdeen 1676-83 and a wealthy trader with Danzig (modern Gdansk), it is a substantial L-plan mansion. Skene carried out extensive alterations, most notably adding oak panelling and fine plaster-work that still survive. In the Long Gallery is a series of tempera paintings of religious subjects (the Annunciation, the Adoration of the Shepherds and the Crucifixion) done in 1622, which show that the Reformation did not take a complete hold in Grampian. The house is now a museum.

Returning to Union Street, the central section is dominated by John Smith's great screen of 1830, an Ionic granite colonnade, 46.8 m long, which gives on to St Nicholas's kirkyard. The location of the burgh's church outwith the medieval boundary of the town is something of a puzzle. The simplest explanation may be that by the time the port of Aberdeen was thriving in the 12th century the Bishop, established on the Don, did not have, or could not acquire, land within the flourishing town. The great length of the kirk impresses first, and the oddly detailed, solid central tower of 1874, replacing a good original. Within the cruciform medieval plan there are now two churches, created in the 18th and 19th centuries, separated by the transepts and crossing which retain their medieval atmosphere. The pillars of the tower and the clerestorey windows are the earliest features, dating from the late 12th century. The transepts contain important memorials; the north (Collison's Aisle) has several, principally one to Provost Davidson who fell at Harlaw (1411), while the south or Drum's Aisle has a Flemish brass to an Irvine of Drum. Although the chancel was completely rebuilt in 1874 and is now a building of 'inspired meanness', the early 15th century lower church survives at the east end, where the ground falls away sharply. The layout of the 'Lady of

extremely ornate version of Edwardian English Perpendicular, a mighty 127 m long and 16 m high, the eye is carried ever upwards by the ranks of buttresses, to be transfixed by an improbable skyline of granite finials, crockets and fretwork, the 'most intricate sculpturing of granite ever attempted'. This facade fronts an earlier quadrangle designed principally by Archibald Simpson (1837-41) of two storeys with a three-storey centre tower. This tower was more than doubled in height by Mackenzie in 1893, who added a tall, airy lantern which rises to a profusion of spirelets that still dominate the Aberdeen skyline. Mackenzie's ship-like Graduation Hall, the Mitchell Hall, has an excellent east window which traces the history of the University. This hall lies behind the Mitchell Tower whose old hall, by Simpson, is now the fan-vaulted lobby both to the Mitchell Hall and to the Anthropological Museum.

Provost Skene's House

*St Nicholas's Kirk rising behind
John Smith's screen*

*St Nicholas's Kirk: apse of lower
church*

Pittye: her valut' gives an impression of what the original east end of the main church would have looked like: with wide side aisles and a small sanctuary in the form of a five-sided apse. The rib vaulting and corbels are particularly fine. This, after the Low Church at Glasgow Cathedral, is 'the finest of its kind in Scotland'. To return to the nave, this was rebuilt in 1751-5 to designs by the Aberdeen-born James Gibbs, the architect of St Martin's in the Fields in London. The pedimented west front is particularly successful; it is 5.4 m further east than the medieval west front. Within, the West Kirk is furnished as the burgh kirk, with galleries around and a grandiose pew for the Lord Provost. In the kirkyard is a tilting sea of green table tombs and some baroque monuments.

Continuing up Union Street, the last fragment of Smith's Trinity Hall can be seen on the opposite side

The Music Hall, formerly the Assembly Rooms

just before crossing Union Bridge. This crosses a great airy space where once the Denburn flowed. One block further on is the Music Hall, built in 1820 as the Assembly Rooms, a club or meeting place for wealthy landowners, to a design by Archibald Simpson. This is a superb example of his Greek Revival style, with a dominant, but restful, six-columned portico. The simplicity is striking; only the sharply cut Ionic capitals and the strong horizontal lines of the cornices relieve the granite ashlar, yet the whole building has a solid grace that is utterly pleasing. The Music Hall was added at the rear in 1858/9; the whole was refurbished lovingly in 1986.

The west end of Union Street became a highly desirable residential area during the 19th century, as the 'quality' moved from their town houses in the older eastern parts of the burgh, such as the Upper Kirkgate, Guestrow, and Shiprow. Bon Accord Square and Crescent, laid out by Simpson in 1823 on the south side of Union Street for the Incorporated Trades, have a real Georgian elegance and spaciousness that is all the more remarkable for being achieved in unadorned granite ashlar.

Returning eastwards down Union Street to Union Terrace and turning left (north), the view across the Denburn valley is dominated by the unusual brick gothic spire of Simpson's Triple Kirks. Built as the Free East, West and South Churches for parts of the congregation of St Nicholas in record time after the Disruption of 1843, brick was used to reduce costs. Nevertheless, its proportions (copying one of the two spires of St Elizabeth's, Marburg in Prussia) ensure that it is a striking skyline feature.

The skyline also features several fine domes. At the head of Union Terrace is the grandiose St Mark's church, built in 1892 by Marshall Mackenzie as the South United Free Church, whose granite dome has been pushed forward almost on top of a Greek portico in a very assertive composition. Its neighbour is the

little copper cupola of His Majesty's Theatre (1906) whose Edwardian interior has been restored exquisitely. Both these buildings front another massive viaduct, built in 1886, and a most arresting bronze statue of William Wallace, on a red rubble granite plinth, by W G Stevenson, 1888. Set back on the natural ground level, just to the east, is Simpson's Infirmary of 1832/9, whose dome contrives to rise above each of three restrained, pedimented, fronts. The most easterly copper dome of the vista is on the Cowdray Hall, part of Mackenzie's Art Gallery complex. The concave colonnaded corner with crouching granite lion is his powerful yet dignified War Memorial of 1923-5. It abuts his Art Gallery (1883), whose exterior is an interesting attempt to introduce colour into a granite building; it balances Gray's School of Art (now Robert Gordon's Institute). Between the two is the entrance to Gordon's College, the centre piece of which, the 'Auld Hoose', is by

Aberdeen: Bon Accord Crescent, Archibald Simpson's austere triumph

Aberdeen: Simpson's brick spire of the Triple Kirks

St Mark's Church and His Majesty's Theatre

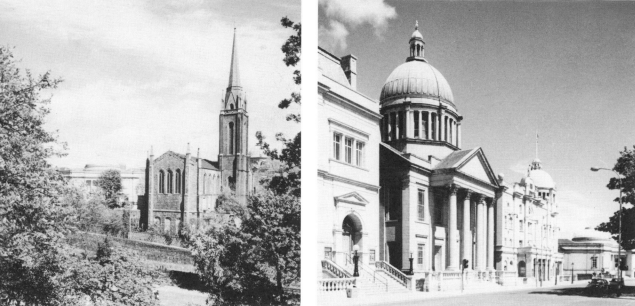

Robert Gordon's College, the 'Auld Hoose' by William Adam

the north. Centred on the Cathedral of St Machar's (no. 48) and the later university at King's College, the Aulton maintained a separate identity from the trading burgh and port on the Dee. This identity still survives, deriving not only from the many old buildings but also from the medieval layout of the burgh itself which still survives in the single street, the High Street, and the narrow lanes that run between the houses, set gable end to the street.

The southern part of the High Street is dominated by the graceful crown of King's College Chapel. The University was founded in 1494 and this was its first building. It remains its finest and most compelling. The gilded foundation inscription beside the west door records that construction began in 1500. The buttresses on the west front bear (from the north) the arms of James IV and his queen, Margaret Tudor, James IV himself, and Alexander Stewart, Archbishop of St Andrews and illegitimate son of the king. The imperial crown rises from a squat, square tower to a height of 31.5 m. When it was rebuilt after having blown down in 1633, a Renaissance termination was added. The fleche in the middle of the chapel roof was releaded in 1655 and bears the initials of Charles I, in honour of the executed monarch.

The chapel is entered from the quadrangle which retains its medieval plan although the other buildings are later. The chapel is aisleless, with an elegant three-sided apse. Large traceried windows fill the north wall, while there are small windows high on the south wall; the access from the sacristy that once stood in the quad to the south can still be seen. The screen, which was moved westward one bay in 1873, the stalls and the ribbed arched wooden ceiling together comprise a unique group of Scottish medieval woodwork. The stalls, probably the work of John Fendour, are each different, with traceried canopies and misericords (ledges on the underside of the tilting seats on which to rest while standing) in a rich, dark oak.

William Adam (c 1731-9). Founded on money made in the Baltic trade, it was intended for the education of the sons of poor burgesses. Now a private school, the central block is plain but balanced, with a statue of the founder above the door and a tripartite spire rising from the middle. On the other side of Schoolhill is James Dun's House of 1769, with good proportions; it is now a museum.

Descending Schoolhill and climbing the Upper Kirkgate brings the walker back to Marischal College. Running north (left) is the Gallowgate, the old route from Aberdeen to the old town or *Aulton*, 1.5 km to

King's College: west end of chapel, tower and quadrangle

King's College Chapel: the great imperial crown spire

King's College Chapel: detail of medieval woodwork of the stalls

King's College: Bishop Elphinstone's memorial (1926)

The great pulpit of St Machar's is here, carved with a blend of medieval and Renaissance elements, while opposite is the 17th century desk of Bishop Patrick Forbes, one of the Aberdeen Doctors, which is lighter and plainer. Between lie the remains of the founder's tomb, William Elphinstone, Bishop of Aberdeen (1483-1514) and Chancellor of Scotland. Despoiled at the Reformation, a black blank slab of Tournai marble remains. The plastered walls and the modern glass by Douglas Strachan complement this most beautiful of university chapels.

A fine recumbent bronze memorial to Bishop Elphinstone, erected 1926, lies outside the west door. Outside the east end of the chapel is an early Christian cross stone found between here and Balgownie, 1.4 km to the north. The buildings immediately north of the chapel, the late gothic New King's and the arcaded Elphinstone Hall were constructed in 1912 and 1929 by Marshall Mackenzie. The spare, square tower in the north-east corner of the quad was built in 1658 and is thus known as the Cromwell Tower.

Old Aberdeen: Grant's Place

Old Aberdeen: the Town House

North of King's the street narrows as the house gables press on to the pavement. Two well restored, but contrasting, lanes are 200 m to the north; nos 1-3 Grant Place are single-storey cottages of 1732 with pantiles, while in the next lane, Wrights' and Coopers' Place, are late 18th century two-storeyed houses. Opposite on the west side of the street in an open area is the old mercat cross, moved from in front of the Town House. This last, in the centre of the street, which opens out to accommodate it and the former market place, is a fine three-storeyed building of granite ashlar, with projecting central, pedimented, bay topped by a small square clock tower and cupola. It was designed by George Jaffray in 1788 and forms a splendidly proportioned centrepiece.

Beyond is the modern world of St Machar's Drive, cut through the Aulton; the line of the High Street continues, however, as the Chanonry. This leads to the cathedral and is lined by the 'manses' of the Professors on sites of the manses of the Cathedral clergy. The 'fortified' cathedral is described separately (no. 48). At the north end of the Chanonry a detour to the west (left) up an old cobbled lane (still with flags for carriages) leads past a possible motte to the Wallace Tower (from 'well house'), which stood in the Netherkirkgate in the port of Aberdeen until 1964. This is a town house of 1610, also called Benholm's Lodging, built on the Z-plan with three storeys. Originally harled, it has a sculpted figure in a recess and the traditional half windows.

A walk of 0.7 km through Seaton Park (entered beside St Machar's) and along the Don leads to the Brig o' Balgownie, completed in 1329, whose strong yet graceful pointed gothic arch rises to 19 m above the river.

Several other notable buildings and structures in Aberdeen are best visited individually, being widely separated. On the south side of Albyn Place, at the west end of Union Street, is the superbly finished

The Wallace Tower (Benholm's Lodging)

Brig o' Balgownie (George Washington Wilson, c 1875)

granite ashlar of Harlaw Academy. Designed by Archibald Simpson in 1837-9 as Mrs Elmslie's Institution for orphan girls, it is of two storeys with projecting pedimented wings and a centre piece of four plain pilasters.

On the south-western outskirts of Aberdeen is the Bridge of Dee, built between 1500 and 1527 and widened on the west side in 1840. Seven semi-circular rib arches with cutwaters give a sense of strength and grace. It was built on the initiative of Bishop Gavin Dunbar and the master of works was Alexander Galloway, rector of Kinkell; the master mason was Thomas Franche. It still bears an impressive array of heraldry, including the arms of Scotland, the Regent Albany, Bishop Dunbar and Bishop Elphinstone. The taking of the bridge after a fierce battle in 1639 left Aberdeen open to the Covenanting forces of Montrose.

Some 2 km downstream is the Wellington suspension bridge, built between 1829 and 1831; the pylons and approaches were designed by John Smith. Beyond the harbour, on the seaward extremity of Greyhope Road towers the white column of Girdleness lighthouse. Built in 1833 by Robert Stevenson (grandfather of RLS) to an innovatory design of two lights, the lower was set at the third floor, whose corbelled gallery can still be seen. On the north side of the harbour, the fisher village of Footdee, laid out by John Smith in 1808/9, still preserves a distinct and attractive atmosphere.

Girdleness lighthouse

Bridge of Dee

Banff

NJ 6864.

The settlement at the west side of the mouth of the Deveron became a royal centre by the end of the 12th century. Its importance to the heritage of Grampian lies in its great abundance of 17th and 18th century buildings, the town houses of many local lairds and prosperous tradesmen. From the south one enters Banff by a fine seven-span bridge, built in 1799 by the engineer John Smeaton for the second earl of Fife, principally as an imposing approach to the new Duff House (no. 2).

Collie Lodge, now in the carpark beside the A 98, was a gatehouse of Duff House. It is a single-storey building of 1836 with a fine Doric portico. From the carpark there is a view of the pleasing symmetrical facade of the old Academy; this is also Greek Revival, the work of William Robertson of Elgin in 1837/8.

Banff is on two levels: High Street, along the old ridge, and Low Street, at the level of the river. One may walk from the carpark along High Street which contains many fine examples of the good work of the Banff Preservation Society. Number 1, on the west side, is typical, being a three-storey, three-window house dated 1764 on the skewput on the south-eastern corner. Its neighbours, nos 3 and 5, are also c 1760. Some 300 m along High Street is Trinity and Alvah church which was built in 1844, by James Raeburn of Edinburgh, as a Free Church. Its tall Ionic portico, harled walls and fine quoins and domed belfry are unusually grand for a Free Kirk.

High Street continues as Castle Street, on the east side of which are the remains of the castle whose ditch and early curtain wall, perhaps of the late 12th or early 13th century, can be seen. An interesting postern gate is in the north wall. The other parts of the castle were removed to build the predecessor of the present house, a two-storey and basement design by John Adam (1749-52), the residence of Lord Deskford.

Banff: Trinity Alvah Kirk

Banff Castle

Banff: St Mary's kirkyard

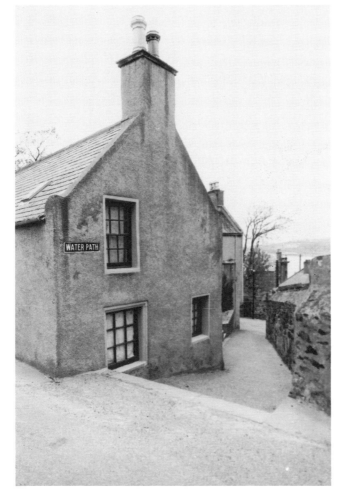

Banff: the Water Path

Banff: 1 High Shore (1675)

The lower part of the town may be reached by the precipitous little Water Path, to the south of the castle, which leads to High Shore. This has the ruins of the late medieval church of St Mary's in a crowded kirkyard on the east side, and several notable buildings on the west. Number 1 High Shore is a 1675 house of two storeys and attic, with neat dormers, a corbelled angle turret and a good sundial at the corner.

Banff: finial of mercat cross

At the north end of High Shore is the harbour, which is of several periods, the original being by John Smeaton in 1770-5. The rubble piers are built in vertically set courses.

West of the south end of High Shore are the Plainstanes, at the north end of Low Street, the heart of the burgh. Here is the ancient mercat cross, 5.9 m high, an unusually well-preserved crucifix on an octagonal foliated capital of early 16th century date, set on a more recent shaft (of 1627/8). It stands in front of the Town House and Tolbooth steeple, which form a fine group, the former of 1764-7, by either John or James Adam, the latter by James Reid, 'squarewright', in 1796. The steeple is in four elegant stages of ashlar, with a pedimented clock face. The Town House is a plain but pleasing three-storey, five-window block.

The Plainstanes, Banff: the mercat cross, Town House and Tolbooth steeple with the Biggar Fountain by John Rhind (1878) in foreground

Banff: Harbour

Elgin
NJ 2162.

The capital of Moray preserves its medieval layout of central street, widening for the town church and market place, and long rigs and pends running off. The soft Moray sandstone produces a mellowness in the buildings, although the light still has the sharpness and clarity of the north.

At the west end of the town, Gray's Hospital in the angle of the Pluscarden and West roads was founded by Dr Alexander Gray, a native of Elgin who made a fortune in India and died in 1808, bequeathing funds for this building. The architect, James Gillespie Graham, between 1815 and 1819 created a bold classical composition of three storeys and a nine-bay pilastered facade. The principal features are a large Roman Doric portico and a great dome and cupola above.

From Gray's, the visitor may descend Old Mills Road to the restored water mill (no. 5) and on to the Bow Brig, the oldest bridge in Elgin, built between 1630 and 1635. East along the High Street is Lady Hill, the medieval castle mound. There was certainly a castle here by 1296, but virtually nothing survives of the castle or of the chapel of St Mary that gave the mound its name. The 25.5 m high column is to George, the fifth and last duke of Gordon and the first Colonel of the Gordon Highlanders (d 1839). The statue of the duke in the robes of the Chancellor of Aberdeen University was added in 1854/5.

In Thunderton Place, to the south of High Street, on the site of the 'Great Lodging' of the Scottish kings, are fragments of Thunderton House, of the early to mid 17th century. The south elevation has four 17th century pedimented dormers with monograms of Duffus, Dunbar and Innes. The low wall of the courtyard incorporates a pair of heraldic beasts. Two stone figures from a doorway are now in Elgin Museum.

The High Street widens gracefully for the central Plainstones or market place which is dominated by Archibald Simpson's great Greek Revival church of St

St Giles, Elgin: Simpson's great portico

St Giles and the Muckle Cross on their island site

Giles (1825-8). This replaced the medieval parish church which was demolished 'because it was old'. The central position of the church means that both ends are equally prominent. Simpson's solution was to site a giant Doric portico at the west end and an eclectic tower, based on the monument of Lysicrates, at the other. This last comprises a square clock tower topped by a delicate open round with a short Corinthian column above. The fine hexagonal pulpit of 1684 from the old St Giles can be seen in P MacGregor Chalmers's excellent, understated St Columba's Church of 1905/6 in Moss Street.

The Muckle Cross, a replica of 1888 of the 17th century cross, stands to the east of St Giles; the lion finial is original.

Numbers 42-6 and 50-52 High Street are excellent examples of late 17th century merchants' houses, which were an important feature of Elgin. The former is dated 1688 and was the Red Lion Inn where Johnson and Boswell ate a 'vile dinner' in 1773. It is three storeys high and has five bays; its principal feature is the arcaded ground floor with five round-headed arches. (The central one leads to a pend.) No. 50-52 dates from 1694 and was for the merchant Andrew Ogilvie and his wife Janet Hay, whose initials are on the skewputs. It has three bays and three storeys with an attic. The arcading on the ground floor is created by short pillars with square capitals. Also known as 'piazzas', these arcaded buildings were sophisticated symbols of their owners' wealth and position. For example, 7 High Street, with three arches

Elgin: 42-6 High Street, formerly the Red Lion Inn

Elgin: 7 High Street, formerly Braco's Banking House

Museum and Little Cross, Elgin

Mackenzie in 1896. This houses the extensive collections of the Moray Society, formerly the Elgin and Morayshire Literary and Scientific Association, founded 1836.

In Greyfriars Street, at the east end of Elgin, is the Convent of Mercy, whose church of 1497, sensitively restored, gives an almost unparalleled impression of a medieval Scottish kirk.

Finally, at the eastern end of Elgin, on East Road, is Anderson's Institution, founded by an Elgin man, Lieutenant General Anderson, who was born penniless and cradled in the cathedral ruins, but who prospered in India. The inscription above the portico reads 'Elgin Institution for the support of old age and education of youth'. This was designed by Archibald Simpson in his Greek Revival style (1830-3) as an H in plan, with recessed Ionic portico and a tall domed belfry above. Although using local sandstone, this building has the severity of Simpson's work in granite.

and a stone slab roof, was from 1703 to 1722 the banking house of William Duff of Dipple and Braco, the progenitor of the earls of Fife (see no. 2).

Just to the east of the former Braco's Banking House is the Little Cross, dated 1733 but with a possibly medieval finial. The original cross was erected in 1402 by Alexander Macdonald to mark the entrance to the chanonry of the cathedral.

Opposite, 1 High Street is the Elgin Museum, a slightly incongruous Italianate ashlar building of 1842 (Thomas Mackenzie), with additions by Marshall

Anderson's Institution, Elgin

2

THE LANDSCAPE OF IMPROVEMENT

Although the improvements of the 18th and 19th centuries had their origin in the enthusiasms of individual landowners, whether for personal economic benefit, or, as was more common initially, for fashionable or even patriotic reasons (wishing to emulate in Scotland practices seen in England), by the mid 19th century wider economic and industrial influences had come to bear. In Grampian the radical changes to the landscape that improvement caused can be seen in five contexts: the great houses and their policies; agriculture; planned settlements; industry and transport.

The houses and their policies

The great houses that were built in Grampian in this period, and those, such as Crathes, Drum or Brodie that continued in occupation, often with additional new buildings, from earlier periods, were the central, controlling, points of often huge estates: in 1879 the earl of Fife still had 103,063 hectares. Such enormous land-holdings had been built up over the centuries by judicious marriages, by inheritance, by timely foreclosure of loans (as did the third earl at Haddo), or outright purchase, either from an impecunious landowner, or, in the case of estates forfeited as a result of their owners' Jacobite activities, from the Commissioners of Forfeited Estates. This last avenue furnished the earl of Fife with the Deeside properties of Balmoral and Dalmore. During the 19th century, in such upland areas as upper Deeside, in particular,

which for centuries had been an important deer forest, the development of sporting lets became a major factor of estate management, and by the end of the 19th century Braemar, in the forest of Mar, had become a fashionable resort for shooting and angling for rich patrons from the south. The fashion had of course been consolidated by the Prince Consort's fondness for such pursuits, conducted on the Balmoral estate which he acquired from the earl of Fife's trustees in 1852.

Prince Albert set about the improvement of the estate with characteristic vigour. His impact in the nine years left to him was considerable, ranging from the new castle by William Smith of Aberdeen, to new bridges, roads, cottages, plantations and a model dairy. Indeed, much of the landscape round Balmoral owes its present appearance to Albert's activities, or to those of his queen and descendants. Not only the Albert Memorial Hall, Ballater (inscription: 'A Prince indeed, and above all titles, a Household Word—hereafter through all time, Albert the Good'), but also the many cairns and other memorials that sit on skylines or nestle in the woods around Balmoral show clearly the firm attachment of the Royal Family to the area.

Further down Deeside, the Glentanar estate and the village of Aboyne are effectively the creations of one man during the 1890s, the Manchester banker Sir William Cunliffe Brooks, who exercised his own principles of landscape design. From a slightly earlier

The planned village of Dufftown, founded 1817

45

The improved landscape of modern Buchan

date the Pitfour estate in Buchan was an even more extravagant private landscape, while in the 1780s the Nottinghamshire landscape architect Thomas White worked at Duff House, Cullen House, Gordon Castle and Castle Fraser.

More utilitarian activities have also stamped whole areas of the north-east with the 'signature' of their particular improving landowner. For example, the meticulous raked drystone dykes of the huge Dunecht estate, or the smaller examples round Pitmedden (no. 18), the tree-belts near Castle Fraser (no. 21), or the much larger scale tree-planting around Haddo House (no. 3) or Darnaway Castle. The story of this last-named important estate in Moray is well presented at the visitor centre at Tearie, 4 km west of Forres (NH 988569).

Agriculture

'Takin't as it is, there's been grun made oot o' fat wasna grun ava; an ther it is, growing craps for the eese o man an beast'.
So mused Johnny Gibb of Gushetneuk, in the splendid novel of the same name, on 30 years of agricultural toil

that helped to create the regular landscape of dyked fields that we see today. What of the earlier farmers and their rigs? Traces of the sinuous high-backed ridges of the pre-improvement cultivation can be found in Grampian, often preserved by an old patch of woodland, now gone, as on the slopes of Hill of Barra, Oldmeldrum (no. 76), visible from the A 947, particularly in snow. The improved fields lie all around. Most of the tenants' money went into them, rather than into their steadings or houses. Never the less, several handsome farmhouses do survive (from the period 1650-1750). Nether Ardgrain, Ellon (NJ 952339) is one of the earliest (1664), but Haddo, Crimond; Birkenbog, Fordyce and Mains of Pittendrum, Pitsligo are also notable. Nineteenth century steadings are now being replaced by multipurpose barns, but those at Bethelnie, Meldrum (NJ 784304) of 1872 and East Lochside, Skene (NJ 793077), with their cart sheds, bothies and slated roofs are typical. The Museum of Farming Life at Pitmedden (no. 18) and the displays at Aden (no. 4) flesh-out the farming practices of the recent past.

Other important farm buildings are the late 17th century Round Square at Gordonstoun (NJ 183688),

A pre-improvement landscape: rigs on the Ythan

An improved steading at East Lochside, Skene

Simple limekiln at Auchindoun Castle

Fragment of the Aberdeenshire Canal at Dyce

the early 18th century kiln barn at Rothiemay (NJ 551484), the horse gin house at Crathes (no. 22), the Sandhaven meal mill (NJ 966672), the windmill stump at Glenglassaugh, Sandend (NJ 560657) and the many dovecotes of varying date throughout the region. Those at Pittendreich, Elgin (NJ 195612), Findlater (NJ 539667), Aberdour (NJ 884643), Fetteresso Castle (NO 843853) and Urquhart Manse (NJ 283626) form a representative selection.

One major factor in the improvement of soil fertility and cultivation was the practice of liming; many local limekilns can be seen in Grampian. For example, there is a string of kilns up Glenbuchat (NJ 367175); a more elaborate one at Pitmedden (no. 18) and a typical rural example at Auchindoun Castle (NJ 348374). Finally, the importance of John Rennie's Aberdeenshire Canal to the improvers cannot be over-emphasised, carrying as it did agricultural implements, tile drains, lime, coals, dung, bark, bones and Peruvian guano into the Garioch. There is a well preserved stretch at NJ 850156. The effect was impressive and is documented, for example in relation to Leith Hall (no. 17). Lord Cockburn, writing in 1838, said,

'I know no part of Scotland so much, and so visibly improved within thirty years as Aberdeenshire. At the beginning of that time, the country between Keith and Stonehaven was little else than a hopeless region of stones and moss, . . . they began, and year after year have been going on, making dykes and drains, and filling up holes with these materials, till at last they have created a country which, when the rain happens to cease, and the sun to shine, is really very endurable.'

In 1839 he wrote, *'Industry can point to no greater triumph than to this part of Scotland called Garioch.'*

The fishing village of Portknockie

Planned villages

Grampian possesses a fine series of planned settlements from the days of improvement. It runs from New Keith (1750, Lord Deskford) and includes Archiestown (no. 7); Laurencekirk (Lord Gardenstone, 1763); Cuminestown (Joseph Cumine of Auchry, 1763); Ballater (Francis Farquharson, 1770); Fochabers (Duke of Gordon, 1776); Huntly (redesigned 1776, by Duke of Gordon); Longside (James Ferguson, 1801); Dufftown (earl of Fife, 1817); Cullen (earl of Seafield, no. 8); Lumsden (1825). All, bar the spa at Ballater (the Pannanich wells), had a combination of agriculture and cottage industry as a motivation. Some, such as the weaving settlement of Laurencekirk, are utilitarian, others are elegant and open, particularly Fochabers which has a fine square with a splendid steepled church by John Baxter as centrepiece.

There were also planned fishing villages, principally Gardenstown (Alexander Garden of Troup, 1720); Macduff (formerly Down, 1783, earl of Fife); Portgordon (duke of Gordon, 1797); Burghead (1805). (Several other fishing villages were the result of earlier, more collective efforts, as at Portknockie (1677) and Findochty (1716), the latter settled by fishermen from Fraserburgh.) One older fishing settlement, Portsoy, was already of wider importance for its foreign trade. A burgh since 1550, its present harbour dates from 1692 and preserves vertically coursed stonework and fine 18th century warehouses such as Corf House (NJ 588662).

Industry

Much remains of the industrial past in Grampian, both inland and along the coast. Quarries were for long important, for granite in particular. The famous Rubislaw Quarry in Aberdeen is now closed; that at Cairngall, Longside was one of the earliest. The slate quarries in the Foudland Hills (NJ 605338) were important sources of roofing slates. Of the ironstone

Slate quarries, Foudland

mine at the Lecht (NJ 238158), the remains that still can be seen are of a high-level lade and a curious building that probably housed the crushing machinery.

Distilling grew to prominence during the 19th century: good interpretative displays and tours are provided at six distilleries on the Speyside Whisky Trail and at Dallas Dhu Distillery, Forres (NJ 035565). The textile industry was also important. Linen was produced at Inverbervie (NO 823734), woollen cloth at substantial mills in Elgin (NJ 225631), Keith (NJ 428514) and in Aberdeen. The bell tower of 1777 that called the weavers to work in Drumlithie can still be seen (NO 786809). The beam engine that drove the Dunecht estate's own woollen mill still survives at Garlogie (NJ 782055).

Although there are many water-powered meal mills scattered throughout the region, few are well preserved; that at East Grange, Kinloss in Moray (NJ 094616) is only recently disused. The water-powered saw and turning mill on the Feugh at Finzean (NO 591916) is a fascinating survival, as is the Bucket Mill further upstream (NO 577912).

There are excellent displays on the fishing industry in the new fishing and maritime museums in Aberdeen and Lossiemouth.

Transport

An interesting series of bridges of both stone and iron survives in Grampian. Of those in stone the two in Aberdeen, Balgownie (NJ 941096) and the Bridge of Dee (NJ 929035) are the earliest, but the little Brig o' Keith dates from 1609 (NJ 427507). Several stone bridges are part of the system of military roads built after the 'Forty-five. The finest, at Invercauld (NO 186909), was built by Major Edward Caulfield in 1752 to carry the road that had crossed the Mounth by the Cairnwell Pass over the Dee and on to Corgarff and Ruthven. Another fine bridge on this route is at Gairnshiel (NJ 294008), a high, long single arch. A well preserved section of the military road leaves the A 939 at NJ 296063 and runs over the hill shoulder to the river and on to Corgarff (no. 25).

Other stone bridges were private initiatives by improving landowners, for example the soaring Bridge of Alvah in the grounds of Duff House (no. 2) or the curious tiered Craigmin Bridge at Letterfourie (NJ 441621). The bridges built in the early 19th century quickly became part of the new system of turnpike roads, for example Thomas Telford's elegant bridge of 1817 at Keig (NJ 617186) or William Minto's functional bridge at Potarch (1814: NO 607973). Many of the tollhouses built on the turnpikes still survive and can be recognised from their characteristic bowed gable jutting towards the road.

Invercauld Bridge: 18th century military engineering

To the early iron bridges dealt with in the guide should be added that over the Dee at Park, Drumoak (NO 796981), built in 1854, which is an impressive double span. It was cast in Aberdeen, as was the series of attractive suspension footbridges that cross and recross the middle reaches of the Dee, eg Cambus o'May (NO 420976), Polhollick (NO 343965) or Abergeldie (NO 287953): these date from 1885 to 1905.

Much can be seen by the walker of the former railway system in the north-east. Parts of the Deeside Line are laid out as footpaths (eg NJ 897030), and the former Buchan line is accessible at NJ 894180, but by far the longest route is on the Speyside Way which follows the old Strathspey Railway-line from Spey Bay to Ballindalloch. At Ballindalloch (NJ 168368) there is an early lattice-girder bridge with iron-truss span (1863) crossing the dark Spey.

Of the region's harbours, one of the earliest, Portsoy, has already been referred to. Mention should also be made of those at Peterhead (NK 137460: south harbour, 1773, John Smeaton; north harbour, 1818, Thomas Telford), Fraserburgh (1807), Stonehaven (Robert Stevenson, 1826), Burghead (1807-10, with granaries by Telford), and of course Aberdeen (north pier is the oldest, by John Smeaton, 1775-81, extended by Telford, 1810-16: interesting control tower; NJ 957057).

Finally, the lighthouses around the region's coast include the earliest to be lit in Scotland: Kinnaird Head, Fraserburgh (no. 16)), Boddam (1827), Girdleness, Aberdeen (1833), Covesea (1846) and Tod Head (1897). The development of the lighthouses shows very clearly the direct relationship that existed between pure science and technology during the 19th century: the bull's eye optics of the Covesea light can now be inspected at close quarters in the Lossiemouth Fisheries Museum.

Park Bridge: 19th century technology

Portsoy: the old harbour

1* Fasque House, Fettercairn, Kincardine and Deeside

Early 19th century AD.
NO 648755. On B 974 1.8 km N of Fettercairn.

Built in 1809, this castellated mansion is in a simple, severe style of Georgian Gothic, possibly designed by John Paterson of Edinburgh. The main block is of three storeys with a larger central bay tower with a Doric portico at its base. This last was added in 1829 when the house was bought by John Gladstone, who had made a fortune from supplying corn to the growing industrial communities of south-east Lancashire. In common with several other north-east landowners he later owned slave sugar plantations in the West Indies and invested in the new railways. He was created a baronet in 1846.

From 1830 to 1851 Fasque was the home of his younger son, WE Gladstone, and there is much memorabilia of the four-times Prime Minister to be seen in the house. However, it is as a superbly organised machine for servicing the hunting and shooting proclivities of Sir John's eldest son and grandson between 1830 and 1914 that Fasque is best viewed. (The latter gentleman and seven of his friends once shot more than 3000 pheasants in one day in 1905.) The house illuminates in extraordinary detail the logistics of life in a wealthy Victorian country house, both above and below stairs. This is partly because nothing was ever thrown out, or so it would seem, by any of the six generations of Gladstones that have lived here.

Much of the ground floor is given over to an efficiently laid-out suite of rooms for the (minimum of) fifteen indoor servants to work in. As well as the gloomy servants' hall, where the middle-rank servants ate, there are a kitchen, vegetable scullery, scullery with larder off, still rooms, a housekeeper's room and the butler's pantry. These rooms are still furnished with a daunting array of equipment: armies of coal scuttles and candle-holders, platoons of bed pans, and waves of water-carriers, all of which the staff had to carry to the guests' rooms. The kitchen is particularly impressive, with a spread of shining copper pans all along one wall.

Above stairs, the interiors generally display a sense of comfortable elegance. The entrance hall is particularly pleasing being bright and deep, with a gleaming, glass-scraped floor leading back to a superb double staircase. This is cantilevered into the wall and has low risers and deep treads so that the visitor appears to soar effortlessly upwards rather than merely ascend. The upper landing is lit from an oval cupola above.

The most interesting rooms are the Business Room, the successor of the Laird's room in earlier great houses, which is arranged as a late Victorian estate owner's room with an excellent four seater 'rent desk'; the bathroom, which contains Sir John's grandiose canopied bath with shower, spray, wave, plunge, cold and hot taps; Sir Thomas's bedroom with a wardrobe that looks like a tomb; and the Library, the collecting of books for which was largely the responsibility of the young WE Gladstone, and which boasts above the shelves a series of inspirational busts of some of the

Fasque House (no. 1)

writers represented below. The bedroom of Mr Gladstone's sister, the confined and depressive Helen, is dark and oppressive.

All this solid comfort was funded from the investments made by the Founder and from the income of the improved farms of the estate's tenants. The nearby Episcopal chapel of 1847 is in an early English style by James Henderson: it was for the family, their servants and tenants.

Duff House (no. 2)

2*   **Duff House, Banff, Banff and Buchan**
AD 1730-39.
NJ 690633. 0.4 km S of Banff.
HBM(SDD).

Of all William Adam's creations, this is the most assertive, the most brash, certainly when compared with the calmness of Haddo (no. 3), which he was also building at this time. The explanation lies in Adam's ability to interpret his client's demands and temperament. In William Braco, MP, one of the richest men in the north-east (as a result of his father's banking business), Adam had a client who was determined to impress, if not daunt, his fellow mortals. Created Lord Braco in 1735 and earl of Fife in 1759, Braco and his descendants were a family in a hurry: 'from bonnet lairds to dukes in 150 years' it has been said. Adam responded brilliantly to his patron's pretensions, giving him a building that is swaggering, vainglorious and intimidating: work began in 1730.

Built in an extravagant baroque style, the house consists of a square block of three storeys and a full basement. It is entered up a double curving staircase. The principal feature of the front is a group of four Corinthian pilasters topped by a sculpture-filled pediment and a balustrade. This block is flanked and oversailed by square corner towers that thrust upwards and outwards from the main facade. The effect is dramatic and reminiscent of some of Vanbrugh's creations. The verticality of the design, to which the pilasters make a major contribution, is emphasised by the isolation of the house. Adam originally intended that pavilions should flank the main block, sitting forward from it and linked to it by curving colonnades. That these were never built was due to a dispute between Adam and Braco in 1736 over the cost of shipping the carved Corinthian capitals from Queensferry. It was still unresolved on Adam's death in 1748. Although the house was roofed by 1739, such was Braco's bitterness that he never lived in

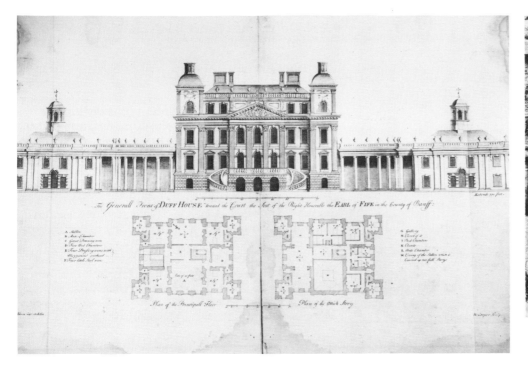

Duff House (no. 2): William Adam's original scheme (1730)

Duff House Mausoleum (no. 2): tomb removed from Banff by the Earl of Fife

it and would draw down the blinds of his coach whenever he passed it.

The visitor should stand before the house on the south lawn and note the overall layout, and details such as the sculpture in the pediment, the lead figures of Mars, Diana and Orpheus above and the urns placed on the balustrade yet higher above. On entering the house the height of the rooms is at once striking and daunting. The delicate plaster ceiling mouldings and the gold leaf on the doors of the first floor are fine rococo work (completed by the second earl), yet for all this refinement the overall effect is strangely lifeless.

The house was eventually occupied by the second earl and his descendants. As part of the break-up of the Fife estates, it was gifted to the burghs of Macduff and Banff in 1906 and its contents sold in 1907. It was used as a hotel, nursing home and army billet, being rescued by the then Ministry of Works in 1956.

Such a grand house had originally a large and impressive park, mostly created by the second earl. Some of the features of this park can still be seen on the riverside walk to the south of the house. There is a fine icehouse and the mausoleum built by the second earl, for which he had two tombstones removed from Cullen kirk (no. 50) and their dates altered to give his family a spurious antiquity. (These stones have since been returned to Cullen, but a third, which he removed from St Mary's, Banff is still against the back wall: it is probably the tomb of a 17th century provost of Banff.) The track winds on to the bridge of Alvah, a magnificent structure of 1772.

3* Haddo House, Tarves, Gordon

AD 1731-6.
NJ 868347. 10 km NW of Ellon, off B 999
Aberdeen/Methlick road.
NTS.

In 1724, the second earl of Aberdeen, William Gordon, in seeking to replace the old House of Kellie at Haddo, whose lands had been in Gordon hands since 1469, obtained a 'draught' from William Adam. It was not until 1731 that work began under the supervision of the Edinburgh mason, John Baxter. The partnership between the pernickity earl, Baxter, and, at a distance, Adam, was not without friction: some details of

Haddo House (no. 3): aerial view

Adam's draught were altered (principally the insertion of a string course) and Baxter complained that he was 'not to expect a great reward, for the peipell in this cuntry knows bravely how to mak ther mony go far'!

The building that was completed in 1735 is a restrained Palladian design on the *Piano nobile* principle, the house integrated with its countryside. It is built in the hard local stone and consists of three blocks linked by curved wings or 'quadrants': the entrance was at first-floor level by way of a small double stair. Some alterations were made by Archibald Simpson in the 1820s when the quadrants were heightened and the parapets added. Major alterations took place in 1879/81, by CE Wardrop, when the original curved stairs to the first-floor entrance were replaced with the present ground-floor entrance hall through the porch and colonnade and considerable redecoration of the interiors was carried out in an early Adam-revival style. The chapel was built between 1876 and 1881 by GE Street, the architect of the London Law Courts.

The most notable rooms are the entrance hall, which has panels painted by John Russell; the Ante-Room, the only room with its original Adam/Baxter panelling, pedimented doorways and Colza oil lamps: it also has a bust of Queen Victoria presented by her to the fourth earl; the Queen's Room, which is light and golden; the Morning Room, with its banana-leaf carpet and view of Giles's garden; the more formal Drawing Room, lined with Van Dykes, a Domenicino and an excellent view of Gight Castle by Giles; the Dining Room and the Library, this last created out of a hay loft in one of the quadrants by the seventh earl, with cedar panelling inlaid with ebony. The Chapel, attached to the north wing, is a calm delight with a barrel roof of light wood and a fine stained glass window by the Pre-Raphaelite Sir Edward Burne-Jones.

The principal apartments overlook a landscape that was deliberately created to delight the eye and to provide entertainment and sport. When George, the fourth earl, came into his inheritance in 1805 he found a treeless waste surrounding a house that had been neglected for 50 years, the third, or 'Wicked' earl having lived away with his three mistresses. However, as that same earl had judiciously increased the estate to 2400 hectares, the means of improvement were to hand. The fourth earl became a zealous improver and is to be remembered for the draining and liming that he promoted and for the cottages, steadings and policies that he created, as much as for his political life which culminated in his unhappy term as Prime Minister from 1852-5 (during which he became embroiled in the Crimean War). With his 80 foresters he planted 14 million trees, while in the 1830s, with the landscape architect and artist, James Giles, he laid out the garden and policies what we see today. Some of the latter are incorporated in the country park that is now run by Grampian Regional Council.

Round Square, Aden (no. 4)

4 Aden House Stables, Aden Country Park, Old Deer, Banff and Buchan

Late 18th/early 19th century AD.
NJ 981479. 0.3 km NE of Old Deer. Enter (by car) off A 950 Mintlaw/Old Deer road.

From the 1750s to 1937 the Russell family built up the estate of Aden to a 4000 ha mix of private policies, farmland and woodland. Since 1975, 92 ha of the former estate have been managed by Banff and Buchan District Council as a country park. Thanks to the work of restoration and interpretation, it is now possible to understand something of life on a major 19th century Aberdeenshire estate.

The principal focus of the park is now the Round Square, once the hub of the Home Farm, which has been restored to its former clean, spare appearance. The harled rubble building, of whose circuit approximately one quarter was never built, dates from c 1800 and is two-storeyed, with six arched cartsheds on the north side. Above the sheds rises a four-storey square dovecote which is surmounted by an elaborate open cupola with 'roman doric' columns. A visitor's centre, with useful interpretative displays, now occupies the cartsheds and also the farm offices in the centre of the square. The North-east of Scotland Agricultural Heritage Centre is also here.

Of particular interest are two small rooms at the east end of the curved block. These were the home of the last horseman and his family; the dark little rooms have been refurnished as they were in the 1930s and now form a vivid and telling contrast with the scale of the whole estate.

Although the mansion house is now ruined, it is possible to visualize how opulent it must have been when occupied. Originally a late 18th century quadrangular building, with a symmetrical south frontage of stepped bays, it was largely reconstructed

Old Mills, Elgin (no. 5)

in 1832/3 by John Smith. The west wing was rebuilt with an outstanding central bow with columns and dome; a *porte cochère* (covered entry for carriages, similar to that at Balmoral) was added asymmetrically to the south front and the court was roofed as a central hall. The west and north lodges of the estate were probably also built at this time, by Smith, the latter having a particularly interesting Greek Revival portico.

Other typical features of a country house and its policies are to be seen, principally the icehouse, lake, and mineral well. There is more conifer planting than would have been the case in the 19th century, but the enclosed feel of the policies can still be had in walking the many footpaths through the grounds.

5*   Old Mills, Elgin, Moray
Late 18th/early 19th century AD.
NJ 206630. In W end of Elgin: turn N off High St/ West Rd at small roundabout in front of Gray's Hospital, down Old Mills Rd for 0.5 km, mills on right.

Although there may have been a mill on this site from as early as the 13th century, most of the present building dates from the 1790s, while the kiln at the north end is from the 1850s. The mill has been restored to full working order by Moray District Council and is now a fine example of a large town mill and ancillary buildings of the age of improvement.

The main block has substantial rubble walls in order to withstand the vibration of the machinery, while the kiln-end is capped by a characteristic pyramidal ventilator. Note the two low breast or undershot water-wheels, on the east and west walls, which are served by the carefully built double lade. On arches spanning the mill lade is a rubble store and cartshed, with a timber upper storey.

6 Consumption Dykes, Kingswells, Aberdeen

Mid 19th century AD.

NJ 862069. 3 km W of Aberdeen, on minor road between the A 944 and the A 96. Turn N off A 944 at Kingswells, and after double bend, stop at fork with farm track. Dyke begins 50 m down track.

Created to 'consume' the rocks and boulders littering the unimproved acres of the estate of Kingswells, which Dr Francis Edmonds had acquired in 1854, this is one of the most impressive monuments of the agricultural improvements in the north-east.

The immense amount of labour that was required to gather the boulders and construct the dyke, 477 m long, 10.5 m wide and 2 m high, becomes clear to anyone walking along the paved central path. With steps up at each end and a water-bay in the middle, this has for long been an object of local pride.

Another, slightly smaller, example lies 200 m to the east (NJ 865061), while the large and curved Rough's Cairn is 1.7 km to the north-east (NJ 877078). However, the 'landstones' were sometimes put to a more elevated use, as in 1857 when the little Gothic Free Kirk at Kingswells itself (NJ 869062) was constructed from field gatherings worked in 'a bold and vigorous manner'.

Consumption Dyke, Kingswells (no. 6)

Archiestown planned village (no. 7)

7 Archiestown, Moray

Late 18th century AD.
NJ 230441. 6 km W of Craigellachie, on B 9102 Craigellachie/Knockando road.

In its rectangular east-west plan and sharp boundary between village and surrounding countryside, Archiestown preserves to an excellent degree the feel of a small planned settlement of the 18th century. It is named after its founder, Sir Archibald Grant of Monymusk, who, in 1760, established what was intended as a community of weavers on the Moor of Ballintomb, a broad shelf above the north bank of the River Spey that was part of the Grant estate of Elchies. The new village burnt down in 1763 and was rebuilt: several of the late 18th century weavers' cottages can be seen on the west and south sides of the square.

Sir Archibald Grant was the son of a law lord, Lord Kames, who, like other judges of his day, had been an enthusiastic improver. The son had been an MP but was expelled from the House of Commons for fraudulent use of charity funds and turned to husbandry and estate improvement for his income. Grant therefore stands apart from many of his fellow early improvers in being driven by economic necessity rather than the dictates of intellectual and social fashion.

The main interest of the village is its tree-lined square, set north-south, at right-angles to the main street. Although many of the buildings on the east and north sides are 19th and early 20th century in date, and the apparent mercat cross is the war memorial of 1920, the whole feel of the village is extremely calm and pleasing, in that the basic unified plan survives. The lanes running at right angles to the High Street, along the plots behind the frontage, also survive and help to pull the plan together.

8   Cullen, Moray

Early 19th century AD.
NJ 5167. On A 98, Banff/Buckie road, 17 km W of Banff.

Of the Cullen that was created a royal burgh in the 13th century but little remains. The old town, which extended from the surviving castle mound (NJ 508670) to the late medieval kirk of St Mary's (no. 50), was by the early 19th century in too close proximity to the Seafield laird's house extensions. Like the duke of Gordon at Fochabers in 1776, the solution was to demolish the village and create a new planned settlement to the east, at some distance from the big house.

Building began in 1821, using a plan of c 1811 that had been modified by Peter Brown of Linkwood. Much of

the detailed building design was carried out by the Elgin architect William Robertson. (The town-plan was further extended, with the addition of the York Place/Seafield Road triangle, in 1825, by the supervisor George MacWilliam from sketches by Robertson.)

The focus of the new town of Cullen, as with other substantial planned towns such as Fochabers or Grantown, is the great square, enlivened in the case of Cullen by being built on a considerable seawards incline. The finest group of buildings within The Square comprises the old Town Hall, Library, Seafield Hotel and garage and 15-19 Seafield Street, on the south-east corner. Built by Col Grant, curator-at-law for the earl of Seafield, as a hotel (cf Monymusk's coaching inn of a slightly earlier date), William Robertson also designed a smithy, stables, a 23.5 ft (7.5 m) diameter council room, courthouse and ballroom. Other pleasing Robertson buildings in the Square are nos 12 and 16 and 23 and 25 Seafield Street. Numbers 2-4 The Square are 1866/7 Georgian survivals, by James Matthews, replacing two houses built in 1822: formerly the North of Scotland Bank, they now form part of the Clydesdale Bank.

The mercat cross in The Square originally stood in the old burgh near the kirk. The cross itself is a 17th century octagonal shaft surmounted by a heraldic beast; it is mounted on a gothic octagon of c 1830, which incorporates a sculptured panel of the Virgin and Child from old Cullen.

Apart from the central square there is another fine group of buildings dating from the first laying-out of the town at 1-3 and 2-4 Grant Street, to the west. With the screen walls and gatepiers they form a symmetrical approach to Cullen House.

However, probably the most immediately striking feature of Cullen is the series of towering railway viaducts that snake between the Seatown by the shore

Cullen (no. 8): old Town Hall in Seafield Square

Cullen (no. 8): Seatown and railway viaduct

and the new town on the brae, thereby stringing together the different elements of the town. Built by PM Barnett for the Great North of Scotland Railway Company as a result of their having been refused permission to traverse part of the grounds of Cullen House, the line was opened in 1886. The westernmost viaduct, over the Burn of Cullen, is the most impressive, being 196 m long and 24.8 m high: it is poised on eight immense arches, while the eastern one forms a prominent feature of the centre of the new town.

To the north of the railway lies Seatown, the fishing community whose houses huddle end-on to the sea beside the harbour. In 1762 there were 29 houses: by 1818, many more. Most of the present houses belong to the later 19th century; in general these are the taller ones with dormers. The harbour was established in 1817, although there had been fishers at Cullen for centuries before that. It was rebuilt during the improvements of 1823. The iron windlass is an important early example of its kind.

9 Glenfiddich Distillery, Dufftown, Moray
Late 19th century AD.
NJ 324410. At N end of Dufftown, on E side of A 941 Dufftown/Craigellachie road.

Before the 19th century the upland areas of the north-east contained many small stills from which illicit whisky was exported over the hill passes to the south. The Glenlivet area, to the south of Dufftown, was a particular centre of this activity, until its owner, the duke of Gordon, instigated legislation in 1823 to suppress smuggling and to permit distilling under licence. The first licensed distillery owner was the former illicit distiller George Smith of Glenlivet; many others were founded in adjacent glens during the 19th century, with the result that Speyside soon became the heartland of Scotch whisky production. Today a signposted 70 mile long trail links six of these distilleries that open regularly for visitors (Monday to Friday, not weekends: from April to September, two all year round).

Glenfiddich, like nearby Glenfarclas (NJ 211381) is open all the year round and is an excellent example of a distillery producing a single malt. Founded in 1887 by William Grant using stills bought from the old Cardow distillery, all the processes from mashing to bottling can be seen. A vivid audio-visual programme introduces the guided tour.

In the Mash House ground malted barley (grist) is heated in a huge vat of spring water to produce wort which is then fermented in the Tun Room in deep, dark foaming vats of Oregon pine. The wash thus produced is piped to the Stillhouse where it is distilled twice in dull copper swan's neck stills (the small size reflects the size of the original old stills bought from Cardow). The liquor is passed through gleaming brass and glass spirit safes which allow the fine 'middle cut' spirit to be retained for maturing for eight years in oak casks in quiet, dark crypt-like bonds. After maturation the whisky is mixed with spring water to reduce it to a drinkable strength and then bottled in the bottling hall. The old Malt Barn in which the barley was germinated and dried, is preserved as a visitor centre.

Glenfiddich Distillery (no. 9)

Glenfiddich Distillery (no. 9): copper stills

10* Tugnet Icehouse, Spey Bay, Moray
Late 18th/early 19th century AD.
NJ 348653. 6 km N of Fochabers on B 9104.
Open June-September at all reasonable hours.

Built at the mouth of one of the most important salmon rivers in Scotland, this vast icehouse was part of a complex salmon-fishing station which is a classic example of investment by an improving landowner in a local industry.

Crouched behind grey shingle ramparts are three brick-vaulted blocks that form the icehouse. Each block contains two subterranean chambers which would have been packed with ice collected in winter from ponds near the shore, topped up with ice 'bree' from the river. The ice would have been tipped in through the doors high in the sides of the vaults; each chamber has a sump in the floor for the water melted from the vault-high ice. During the netting season salmon would have been stored in the icehouse, prior to being packed in ice for the journey south, initially by sea, latterly by rail. This was a large operation, employing fishers, overseers, coopers and others to a total of 150 at the end of the 18th century. A substantial manager's house, a store and boiling house (1783) also survive.

The icehouse has been restored by Moray District Council and now houses good displays on the salmon fishing, wildlife and the former boat-building industry of Kingston, north of Garmouth on the opposite bank, founded by men from Kingston-upon-Hull in 1784, using timber floated down the Spey from the forests of Rothiemurcus, Glenmore and Strathspey.

11 Bridge of Dye, Strachan, Kincardine and Deeside
Late 17th century AD.
NO 651860. 10 km S of Banchory on B 974
Banchory/Fettercairn road (Cairn o'Mount).

In a pre-improvement landscape where roads were scarcely cart tracks and hill roads, such as that ascending the Cairn o'Mount between the old town of Kincardine (now gone) and Strachan on the Feugh, merely hill paths, the Bridge of Dye must have been a welcome and imposing sight.

Built in 1680 with a ribbed single arch that harks back to late medieval times, this is one of the earliest bridges in the north-east. Its importance, and that of the north–south routeway on which it stands, are emphasized by an act of 1681 that permitted tolls to be levied for its upkeep.

Tugnet Icehouse (no. 10)

Bridge of Dye (no. 11)

Well of the Lecht (no. 12)

12 Well of the Lecht, Kirkmichael, Moray

Mid 18th century AD.
NJ 234151. On A 939 Cockbridge to Tomintoul road, c 2 km N of the summit of the Lecht. Park at picnic site at foot of long hill and cross road to well.

Above a small natural spring a white stone plaque, dated 1754, records that five companies of the 33rd Regiment built the road from here to the Spey. This marks one section of the military road system that extended control over the Highlands after the 'Forty-five. From Ruthven Barracks on the Spey near Aviemore, the road climbed the Lecht and ran southwards by the garrisoned Corgarff Castle, across Gairnshiel Bridge, then over the Dee by Major Caulfield's majestic Invercauld Bridge, on past the garrison in Braemar Castle, and south over the Cairnwell Pass to Blairgowrie and Perth. The well is small but the undertaking vast.

13 Craigellachie Bridge, River Spey, Craigellachie, Moray

Early 19th century AD.
NJ 285451. 0.3 km W of Craigellachie, off A 941 Craigellachie/Rothes road.

'The bridge is of iron, beautifully light, in a situation where the utility of lightness is instantly perceived. The span is 150 feet, the rise 20 from the abutments, which are themselves 12 above the usual level of the stream.' (Robert Southey, *Journal of a Tour of Scotland in 1819*).

Probably the oldest surviving iron bridge in Scotland, and one of the finest in Britain, this is one of Thomas Telford's most spectacular creations. A single four-ribbed arch of cast-iron with a span of 45.7 m, it leaps the swift Spey, springing from abutments of rustic ashlar topped by cylindrical crenellated turrets.

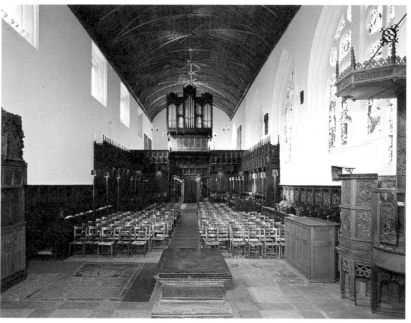

*Provost Ross's House, Shiprow,
Aberdeen*

King's College Chapel

*Telford's iron bridge, Craigellachie
(no. 13)*

Haddo House (no. 3): the Lobby or Ante Room

It was built between 1812 and 1815 as part of the overall improvement of the Highland road system then in progress under the direction of the Commissioners for Roads and Bridges, who put up half the £8200 cost. It was a vital crossing of the Spey, midway between Fochabers and Grantown, where the river is contained by the hard rock of the north bank. (This crag had to be cut back for the approach.)

The Commissioners' engineer, Thomas Telford, built in iron springing from tall abutments in order to accommodate the ferocious rise to which the Spey in flood is prone; the arch survived the devastating flood of 1829. The masonry abutments were the work of Telford's assistant, the Shrewsbury builder John Simpson, while the ironwork was cast at Plas Kynaston in the vale of Llangollen in Denbighshire by William Hazeldine ('Merlin' Hazeldine to Telford). The iron ribs then had to be floated over Telford's other extraordinary work, the Pontcysyllte aqueduct on the Llangollen canal and shipped round to the Moray Firth and up the Spey.

Telford's Craigellachie Bridge
(no. 13)

Brunel's Balmoral Bridge, Crathie
(no. 14)

14 Balmoral Bridge, Crathie, Kincardine and Deeside

Mid 19th century AD.
NO 263949. Carries the B 976 across the Dee from the A 93 at Crathie, 10 km W of Ballater. Park in public carpark on N side.

This bridge was commissioned by Prince Albert in 1854 as part of the improvements then being carried out on the newly acquired Balmoral estate. It altered the route of the public road through the estate, thereby creating more privacy, and was intended as a more solid substitute for the typical Deeside suspension bridge 0.8 km downstream (NO 266942). The Prince Consort turned to the designer of the great Royal Albert Bridge over the Tamar in Devon, the renowned engineer, Isambard Kingdom Brunel, who designed a novel, single-span, wrought-iron plate-girder bridge with diamond-shaped perforations in the girder web.

This is probably the earliest bridge of its type in Scotland. The two riveted girders are almost unique in Brunel's work, the closest parallel being in a girder designed for the East Bengal Railway. The girders are mounted on two large piers of local granite, have a

span of 39.8 m and support a 4.1 m wide deck of pine planking and tarmac. The iron-founder was R Brotherhood of Chippenham, Wiltshire (three of his name-plates survive on the bridge) and the building of the piers was supervised by Dr Andrew Robertson, the doctor and factor at Balmoral. It was completed (after delays in building the piers) in 1857.

In the event, what was to Brunel a bridge of 'functional elegance' and 'perfect simplicity' did not please the Royal Family. The Queen's journal, normally so effusive about any new bridge or building, or any Albert-led improvements to her 'Dear paradise', is ominously silent on the bridge literally at her gateway. There is certainly nothing baronial, gothic or romantic about it, and the Queen's taste inclined that way. As a result it was omitted from Brunel's canon and largely ignored. However, it is an important example of his work.

Speymouth railway viaduct (no. 15)

15 Speymouth Railway Viaduct, Urquhart, Moray

Late 19th century AD.
NJ 345641. 5 km N of Fochabers; part of Speyside Way. Approach (by car) on B 9104 Fochabers/ Spey Bay road, carpark signposted to W just after Bogmoor.

Built by Blaikie Bros, Aberdeen, in 1886 for the Great North of Scotland Railway between Elgin and the Banffshire coast, to a design by Patrick Barnett, this is an awe-inspiring iron structure thrust between river and sky.

Its great length (290 m overall) was determined by the Spey's habit of periodically changing channels in the broad level plain near its mouth. The solution was to build a great bowed central truss, 106.6 m long and 13 m high, with three 30.5 m plain truss approach spans on either side, all supported on circular ashlar piers with granite capitals. When completed the bridge was tested with a load of 400 tons of gravel in 20 trucks; the bridge deflected by 29 mm.

Now part of the Speyside Way from Spey Bay to Ballindalloch, the walker on the bridge can fully appreciate the confidence of Victorian engineering in erecting this cathedral of grey girders and trusses that arch above the ceaseless, turbid Spey.

Speymouth railway viaduct (no. 15): a girder tracery

Kinnaird Head Lighthouse (no. 16) and Wine Tower by William Daniell

16*   Kinnaird Head Lighthouse, Fraserburgh, Banff and Buchan

Late 18th century AD.
NJ 998675. At N end of Fraserburgh; turn N off High Street (A 98) up Barrasgate Road and Castle Terrace.

One of the first tasks of the Commissioners appointed under the act of 1786 . . . *for erecting Certain Lighthouses in the Northern Part of Great Britain* was to seek a site on the most northerly part of Aberdeenshire, the north-east corner of the mainland. The tower-house built in the 16th century by Sir Alexander Fraser, eighth laird of Philorth, proved to be in an ideal spot and to provide a ready made elevated platform, four storeys high. By converting the cap-house of the turnpike stair the engineer Thomas Smith achieved a simple lantern chamber which was first lit on 1 December 1787, thereby becoming the first lighthouse in northern Scotland.

Originally the light was fixed, coming from banks of whale-oil lamps each with its own mosaic of mirror glass behind; in clear weather that light could be seen from 12 or 14 miles away. The lantern was rebuilt and upgraded in the 1820s and again in 1851. It now comprises a short circular tower with a domed lantern set with triangular panes of glass. The first permanent radio beacon was established here in 1929.

The usual flat-roofed, white-washed keepers' houses and stores form a small but windy courtyard at the base of the tower.

Above the rocks 100 m to the east is another 16th century tower, the Wine Tower. Although now truncated, it contains one chamber with important heraldic bosses which are paralleled at Crathes (no. 22).

3

BARONIAL RESIDENCES

Until the time of the industrial revolution and the building of factories, lighthouses, bridges etc, the Grampian landscape would have been dominated by the buildings erected by the church in its various guises, and by the ruling class, whether as agents of royal authority, or, later, as competitors in the display of wealth and power through architectural sophistication.

One of the great richnesses of Grampian is the range of fortified buildings which still survives. Representatives of nearly every type or stage in the tradition can be found. Several thrust themselves to notice by virtue of their completeness or style. The sequence begins in the 12th century with the simple but domineering earthen mounds or mottes bearing timber towers, such as Duffus (no. 32), which were erected as part of the extension of feudal power. The exact dating of the earliest stone castles is controversial, but by the early 14th century, several important castles had been constructed, most of them castles of enclosure with stone curtain walls, such as Kildrummy (no. 30) or Balvenie (no. 29). A separate tradition is represented by the towers, with vaulted chambers one on top of the other. The castle of Dunnideer (no. 75), c 1260, and the great Tower of Drum (no. 31), begun in the late 13th century, are among the earliest in this long-lived tradition in Grampian. In castles of both traditions the focal point was the great hall or chamber where the lord held court, ate and entertained; his private chamber would

'The castle reveals itself turrets-first': the imposing north front of Castle Fraser (no. 21)

be close by. The courtyard castle permitted these rooms to be on a single level, the so-called palace or palatial plan, seen at Balvenie, Kildrummy and Fyvie. In the towers a vertical separation took place initially, as at Drum. However, the development of a more elongated plan, as seen in the Z-plan, ie with towers built at the opposing corners of the central block, permitted these apartments to be on one level, as at Castle Fraser (no. 21) or Brodie (no. 19). By the 17th century the dictates of defence were decreasing; the end of the tradition is represented by Leslie Castle (NJ 599248) of 1661, as much a house as a fortalice.

Such is the richness of Grampian in castles that there is space for only a passing mention of such as Braemar, with its Hanoverian refortification (NO 156923), Coxton, a tower almost in miniature (NJ 261607), Muchalls with its excellent plasterwork (NO 891918), Towie Barclay's impressive vaulted hall with oratory (NJ 744439), Pitcaple (NJ 727260), the Wine Tower, Fraserburgh with its heraldic bosses (NJ 999675), Auchindoun's wild and lofty ramparts of an earlier timber phase (NJ 348374), Findlater's cliff-side eyrie (NJ 541672), the splendid oak hammerbeam roof of Randolph's Hall at Darnaway (NH 994550), the hall house at Raemoir (NO 694994) and the related sites of Rothes (NJ 276489), Kindrochit (NO 151913) and Boharm (NJ 310451), the enclosure at Coull (NJ 512022), or the mottes of Cullen (NJ 508670), Durris (NO 779968), Inverugie (NK 102486), Strachan (NO 657921) and the Bass of Inverurie (NJ 780205).

The simple earthen motte of Cunningar, Midmar

Ecclesiastical power: the palace of the Bishops of Moray at Spynie

These castles and towers encompass nearly three-quarters of a millennium of architectural innovation and express various forms of control, authority and prestige. They also represent great social changes. Initially, the medieval earthen mottes and stone castles of enclosure were either erected by the king (eg the first phase of Kildrummy, no. 30) or a great baron who had been granted the right to build by the king (eg Freskin at Duffus, no. 32). More rarely, the power of the church is seen, as in the towering walls of the 15th century bishop's palace of Spynie (NJ 230658). Latterly, by the 16th century, the break-up of church lands provided one avenue by which wealth and the architectural sponsorship that it made possible could be acquired (eg Crathes no. 22). By the early 17th century the rise of a new type of baron from the class of rich merchants and lawyers led to more patronage. Indeed, that the royal arms in an overmantel in the palace of the first marquis of Huntly (the Cock o' the North) were less fine than those prepared for the merchant Danzig Willie at Craigievar has been seen, perhaps fancifully, by one historian as a symbol of the triumph of 'honest trade over feudal privilege'.

The late 16th and particularly the 17th and 18th centuries were very much the time of such new lairds as the two William Forbeses of Tolquhon and of Craigievar. These men were leaders, organisers and arbiters in their baronies; they enjoyed a curious amalgam of 'property, privileges, authorities and obligations'.

Grampian's baronial residences can provide the visitor with a sense of contact with the past that is in some cases immediate and vivid. Such experiences are perhaps best expressed in terms of levels of light and shade. In the old tower of Drum one can sit on a stone window seat bound within the massive wall of the upper hall and observe the sunlight trying to pierce the dark dry dustiness of that huge medieval space. Three hundred years younger than Drum, the painted rooms of Crathes are quiet and free in comparison; their ceilings in the dim, even light parade, admonish and entertain. By the late 18th century the light is full and clear and seen best in the comfortable regency elegance of the oval drawing room of Leith Hall; it is of universal appeal.

17* Leith Hall, Kennethmont, Gordon

AD 1650–1900.

NJ 540297. 10 km S of Huntly, off B 9002 Insch/Huntly road.

NTS.

Leith Hall was in the same family, the Leiths and Leith-Hays, for 300 years. The house forms a pleasing whole, built of four wings on a square, like a modest chateau, but with a complex architectural history as a result of the additions of successive lairds.

The modern visitor approaches the west and most recent wing; to the left (north) is the oldest wing, built in 1650 as a plain rectangular turreted block with a courtyard and laich biggins (brew-house, bake-house, stores and stables) to the south. (There is an excellent NTS guidebook with useful reconstructions of the different phases.) Conventional and unadorned, this block had none of the exuberance of Craigievar or Castle Fraser which date from the more peaceful times at the beginning of the century.

In 1756, John Leith, the fourth laird, built up the east wing, re-sited the stables (the curved block to the north), inserted kitchens on the south side and added little pavilions at each corner. This house had, for its time, the inconvenience of looking into the kitchen courtyard. Around 1797 General Alexander Leith-Hay instituted major changes, turning the house back to front and creating a new south wing for the principal apartments. These five provincial Georgian rooms are the best in the house, particularly the oval Drawing Room, the Dining Room and the Library. In heightening the east wing he also added little turrets to the south wing to harmonise with those on the original north wing. In 1886 the Billiard Room was built above the arch to the courtyard on the west side by the eighth laird, Alexander Sebastian. This was later

Leith Hall (no. 17), from SE

changed to a Music Room; drum turrets were also added to the north-west and south-west corners and the projecting entrance hall at the east.

A major element of Leith Hall's appeal is the quantity of objects, paintings and furniture that relate directly to the various lairds. For example, in the Dining Room that he created is a portrait of General Alexander Leith-Hay, the sixth laird, with whom the family's fortunes revived, thanks to his Jacobite uncle Andrew Hay of Rannes and a cousin who left him a sugar plantation in Tobago which he sold for a not inconsiderable £29,000. The pardon that Andrew Hay eventually received from George III in 1780 as an act of 'compassion of our special grace' can be seen in the Library, along with Prince Charles Edward Stewart's shagreen writing case. There is also much military memorabilia; three lairds, the sixth, seventh and eighth, saw service overseas, so a characteristic sample of much of British imperial history is preserved here, including Col Alexander Sebastian's booty from the sacking of Oudh.

Several lairds were improvers, albeit not in the van of the movement. The fourth laird, John, built the curved stables (which are not unlike the Aden Round Square, no. 4); his second son, General Alexander Leith-Hay, took advantage of the opening of the Aberdeenshire Canal in 1805 to send carts to Inverurie for lime. He also introduced (40 years after Grant of Monymusk) potatoes, pease, turnips and clover.

In the policies, the walled garden, largely created by the second last laird, contains two important Pictish symbol stones, notably the Wolf stone from Percylieu. The garden opens through a delightful 19th century Moon Gate on to the old turnpike road that ran over the hill to Huntly. To the south-east of the house are two ponds created for boating, fishing and duck shooting and an icehouse, the Victorian country house refrigerator.

18* The Great Garden of Pitmedden, Pitmedden, Gordon

Late 17th century AD.
NJ 885280. 7 km E of Oldmeldrum, signposted N off A 920 Oldmeldrum/Ellon road c 0.5 km W of Pitmedden village.
NTS.

When King James VII met opposition among the Scottish law lords to his catholicism, one of the Lords of Session that he had removed from the bench was Alexander Seton, Lord Pitmedden. Seton retired from public life to pursue a major project that he had begun in 1675, the creation of a formal or 'great' garden. A date-stone recording the garden's foundation (*Fundat 2 May 1675*) can still be seen in the garden wall, the initials standing for Sir Alexander Seton and his wife, Dame Margaret Lauder. In creating a large formal garden, 145 m square, with two main sections on different levels, Seton was following a well-established English pattern.

Seton's garden consisted of an upper and lower enclosure, divided by a wall with pavilions to north and south. The lower garden contained four large rectangular borders or parterres, ornamented with box hedging, which were viewed from terraces to north and south, and elegant garden furniture such as fountain and sundial. The restoration of the garden since 1952 was designed by Dr J S Richardson and others and carried out by the Trust's head gardener (the Beechgrove gardener), George Barron.

Three of the parterres follow designs shown on Gordon of Rothiemay's 1647 view of the Palace of Holyroodhouse, while the fourth, in the south-west, contains the arms of Sir Alexander Seton. The legends *Sustento Sanguine Signa* (With blood I bear the standard) and *Merces Haec Certa Laborum* (This sure reward of our labours), the bleeding heart in the centre of the arms and the 17th century soldier on the pavilion weather vanes all refer to the death of Seton's

The Great Garden of Pitmedden (no. 18)

father, John, fighting on the royalist side against the Covenanters at the Bridge of Dee in Aberdeen in 1639.

In the middle of the lower garden is a fountain containing seven stones from the cross fountain in Linlithgow and three from Pitmedden; they were possibly all cut by Robert Mylne for the restoration of Charles II. The pavilions are two-storeyed garden shelters with ogee roofs very similar to one at Bruce's Kinross House. In the upper garden is a herb garden,

for cookery, perfume and medicine, and another fountain, Sir Alexander's own.

Another feature of Pitmedden is the Museum of Farming Life, with farmhouse and ancilliary buildings containing an important collection of 19th and early 20th century farming implements. The dark, cold little Bothy gives a good impression of the living conditions of the hired help a generation or so ago. Across the road is an excellent example of an estate limekiln and quarry pit of the early 19th century.

19* Brodie Castle, Forres, Moray
16th–19th centuries AD.
NH 979577. 5 km W of Forres. Signposted to N off A 96 Forres/Nairn road just E of Brodie. NTS.

There have been Brodies at Brodie for over 800 years; 25 lairds in all, although the present building dates only from 1567, the time of the 12th laird, Alexander. The first structure was a standard Z-plan tower-house, a rectangular block with square projecting towers at two opposite corners. The south-western tower and the main block occupy the western half of the south front. Early in the next century a west wing was added, lying to the north of the south-west tower and hard against the main block. In the 19th century a two-bayed east wing was built, immediately to the east of the original tower.

The 16th century tower-house was a compromise between comfort and modest security. The latter can be seen in the vaulted guard-chamber at the base of the south-western tower with its gun-loops and slit windows. The principal apartments, where comfort could be had, would have been on the first floor. The high hall, which occupied the whole of the main block, is now the Red Drawing Room, a ponderous conversion by William Burn in the 1820s, while the laird's private chamber, which was in the adjacent south-western tower, is now the remarkable Blue Sitting Room. The original vault survives here, covered in rather crude plasterwork of the 1630s.

The addition of the west wing in the early 17th century provided on its first floor a large room for the laird's use adjacent to the old laird's room. This room is now the Dining Room. The visitor may not immediately appreciate that the dusky brown maidens

Brodie Castle (no. 19), from SW

Brodie Castle (no. 19): detail of dining-room ceiling

and vines that spill from the blue background of the ceiling are made of plaster; the graining was applied by the factor in the 1820s who felt that he was creating a room that would be 'perfectly unique'. It is difficult both to interpret and to date the plasterwork. The four groups of emblematic maidens in the corners may represent the elements earth, air, fire and water. There are a few late 17th century parallels, however, which would place it in the lairdship of either of two intensely Presbyterian lairds. The 19th laird, Alexander (1697-1754), is altogether the more lively and likely candidate.

His wife, Mary Sleigh, was responsible for a major remodelling of the grounds with radiating avenues, a short canal and pond and a wilderness. Like many early improvers, she and her husband ran into financial difficulties; however, the essential elements of their work still survive in the west end of the present avenue and the pond.

The last phase of building at Brodie began in 1824 when William Brodie, the 22nd laird, commissioned an elaborate scheme from William Burn of which only the east wing was built. In 1846 the York architect James Wylson carried out various modifications, including the remodelling of the entrance hall with squat 'Romanesque revival' columns and the fitting out of the pleasing library.

The paintings at Brodie represent a particularly wide collection and include a large number of 20th century artists collected by the 24th laird.

A fine Pictish stone, Rodney's Stone, stands beside the entrance drive. Found at the church of Dyke, it has a cross on one side and two fish monsters, a Pictish beast and a double disc and Z-rod on the other, all carved in relief. It also bears three ogam inscriptions, one of which (to the right of the cross) transliterates EDDARRNON; the name *Ethernan* is recorded in the *Annals of Ulster* referring to a Pict who died in AD 669.

Craigievar Castle (no. 20): from NE

20* Craigievar Castle, Alford, Gordon
Early 17th century AD.
NJ 566094. 7 km S of Alford on A 980 Alford/
Banchory road.
NTS.

Dating from a time of relative peace and confidence, after the strife of the Reformation and before the Covenanting troubles, Craigievar has immense assurance and lightness. The castle has survived, through good fortune and sensitive stewardship, largely untouched since 1626, with the result that a visit becomes a highly rewarding journey back to the 17th century. There are few so authentic experiences, in which the architecture, decoration, furnishings and even the smells of woodsmoke and resin of a building unite, than a visit to this, the most serene of Scotland's many castles.

Craigievar was the product of a new type of laird, the cultured Scot who was also successful in the Baltic trade. William Forbes, otherwise known as 'Danzig Willie' or 'Willie the Merchant', was the second, and initially impecunious, son of the laird of Corse near Lumphanan. He attended Edinburgh University, made a good bourgeois marriage to the daughter of a provost of Edinburgh, Marjorie Woodward, and prospered in the trade with northern Europe, mainly Danzig (Gdansk). He did so well that his epitaph claimed
   'The toil of others to obtain wealth was . . .
   . . . to him a pastime.'
At any rate, by 1610 he could purchase the partly built castle at Craigievar from the Mortimer family and supervise its completion according to his own distinctive taste.

Craigievar today rises alone out of the gentle brae, six storeys of soft pink harl, smooth and plain up to the fourth floor, thereafter a broken riotous skyline of corbelled turrets, ogee-topped towers, crown-like balustrades and serrated gables. Originally it stood in

Craigievar Castle (no. 20): upper works

Craigievar Castle (no. 20): the Great Hall, looking to the screens

joyful spirit of the Renaissance, translated into a uniquely Scottish architecture, called Scots Baronial, of which Craigievar is the crowning achievement. It is generally accepted that this was the work of one of the Bell dynasty of master masons who built Castle Fraser and Midmar, possibly I (John) Bell. The castle was completed by 1626.

The design of the interior is no less skilful, there being the remarkable, in view of the narrowness of the tower's base, total of nineteen apartments. Of these, the great hall on the first floor is one of the finest rooms of any period in Scotland and is little altered in 360 years. At once medieval and Renaissance in feel, it is altogether entrancing. Its basic structure, a rectangular hall with a four-part groined vault, wooden screens and gallery, is medieval in inspiration, but the plasterwork which clads the vault in a riot of strap work, portrait medallions and elaborate decorative pendants is like the ceiling of an Elizabethan country house. The major feature of the hall, the great fireplace, is of Gothic proportions, surmounted by a vast plaster Royal Arms and supporters, the whole flanked by classical caryatids. (Willie the Merchant was allowed to display the Royal Arms—in their proper Scottish quartering—as he was a tenant in chief of the king and could exercise justice on the King's behalf on his lands.) Painted and gilded, this centrepiece would have added drama to the sittings of the Barony court. The plasterwork on the vault was done in 1626 by itinerant English craftsmen using moulds that were also used at Bromley by Bow, Glamis and Muchalls. The bowed oak door in the north-western corner leads to the private stairs to the laird's bedroom.

The other main apartment on this floor, the Withdrawing Room, is a fitting contrast to the hall. Panelled in *Eastland boards* of Memel pine the 1625 ceiling is low but also highly decorated, Queen Margaret of Scotland (1057-93) being the central motif.

the north-eastern corner of an enclosing barmkin, of which an ivy-clad fragment survives to the west of the tower.

In plan, the castle consists of two blocks arranged in an L, with a small square tower in the angle. The single door is in the small angle tower and is thus protected. The top third of the castle is projected out on an ornate corbel-table supporting unusually large (two-storeyed) turrets. It is adorned with crowstepped gables and grotesque masks (concealing shot-holes) and decorated water spouts as well as ogival-roofed rounds and almost classical balustrades. This is the

The second floor contains only the Tartan Bedroom, with fine plasterwork even in a tiny dressing room off, as the vault of the hall occupies the main tower at this level. On the third floor is the main or Queen's bedroom, to which the private stair leads from the dais end of the hall. The Blue Room, on the floor above, is more spacious, the walls now being corbelled out. Many of the twenty-four shot-holes are at this level, in the turrets. The fifth floor contains another notable room, the Long Gallery, which would have been used as a promenade in poor weather, for some sittings of the Barony court or as a grand reception room, originally richly decorated with heraldry and pictures.

Above all these interlocking rooms, a narrow stair leads to the roof of the little square tower. Here, six storeys up, is a fine solid platform with an elegant balustrade which overtops even the turrets and gablets; only the splendid gilded weather cock of the Forbeses on the adjacent ogee is higher.

Castle Fraser (no. 21): the great corbel table and turrets

21* Castle Fraser, Kemnay, Gordon

Mid 15th–early 19th centuries AD.
NJ 722125. 7 km SW of Kintore, on back road between Dunecht (on A 944) and Kemnay (on B 993). Signposted.
NTS.

As a traveller of old, the modern visitor approaches Castle Fraser from the north, down a gentle tree-lined slope, so that the castle reveals itself gradually, turrets first. It is thus really only when the visitor is standing on the level ground beside the castle, which now soars above him, that the full scale of the building is appreciated. The five main building campaigns can be discerned by viewing the castle from the south-west (the angle of the colour photograph).

The earliest part of the structure is the remains of the rectangular tower that was probably built in the middle of the 15th century by Thomas Fraser. This was a smaller version of the Tower of Drum (no. 31), 11.9 m by 9.9 m; it is now represented by the eastern two thirds of the ground and first floors of the central block on the south side. The entrance to this tower can be seen in the north wall of the hall on the first floor, immediately west of the blocked recess in the middle of the wall. In 1565, the fifth laird, Michael Fraser, and the mason Thomas Leiper (who was later to work at Tolquhon, no. 26) began to build a square tower at the north-western corner of the old block (this is the Michael Tower, the westernmost harled tower) and a round tower at the south-east corner, thus creating a modest Z-plan manor house. Both towers were taken to the level of the crown of the hall vault, ie the third floor. The entrance to this building would also have been at first-floor level, and is represented by the blocked recess in the centre of the north wall of the hall.

In the three decades before 1618, under the guidance of John Bell, one of the famous dynasty of north-east master masons, the manor house was transformed by

Castle Fraser (no. 21): the great hall (former castle entry on left)

Andrew Fraser. The west gable of the original central block was demolished and rebuilt 3.1 m to the west. (The join is visible in the hall, while the exterior of the new west wall has been stepped in twice to clear the south windows of the Michael Tower, the south-east corner of which was demolished.) Two storeys were added to the Michael Tower and no fewer than four to the Round Tower, while the central block was also heightened. At the fourth-floor level a pronounced corbel table was built right round the building, stepping down at the new two-storeyed rounds and containing exuberant false stone cannon and cable moulding. On the north side a 'sumptuous frontispiece' containing the Fraser arms below the Royal arms was set in a richly carved frame; it may have been carved by the mason who did the Huntly doorpiece (no. 27). Originally gilded, it is a confident assertion of baronial splendour.

After 1618, Andrew Fraser, by now Lord Fraser, carried out further building; a kitchen with room above (the present Dining Room) was built against the north-east

corner of the main block and then two wings of laich biggins were built running north from the castle to form the present courtyard.

Little was done to the castle in the 160 years between Lord Fraser's death in 1636 and Miss Elyza Fraser's inheritance of it. It is likely that her only alteration was the insertion of the present heavy, classical entrance in the middle of the south front (see no. 41). However, the impact of her great-nephew, Col Charles Mackenzie Fraser was altogether more far reaching. From 1814 he began 57 years of change which destroyed most of the early interiors; mercifully, the patient work of the earlier 20th century owners removed most of his additions, apart from the present library, created by John Smith of Aberdeen.

Of the interiors, the Laigh Hall has its fine 15th century vault, the High Hall is much altered but preserves the old entrances, while the oratory and Priest's or Bailiff's room in the Michael Tower preserve something of the feel of the 17th century.

Crathes Castle and gardens (no. 22)

Crathes Castle, Banchory, Kincardine and Deeside

Late 16th century AD.
NO 734968. 3 km E of Banchory, signposted N off A 93.
NTS.

The great L-plan tower-house of Crathes is an excellent example of the changes in fortune which certain families achieved during the 16th century through the appropriation of church lands. The Burnett family had been in the Banchory area since the early 14th century, as hereditary keepers of the Forest of Drum, living in a thoroughly medieval style on the dank crannog or lake dwelling at Leys (north-east of Banchory). The marriage arranged in 1543 between Janet Hamilton, daughter of Canon Hamilton of the abbey of Arbroath, and Alexander Burnett produced a sizeable dowry of church lands which enabled work to begin on a stylish new tower at Crathes.

The work, which took intermittently from 1553 to 1596, was carried out by one of the great Bell family of masons. Each wall face is different, the creamy pink harling rising to a deep corbel-table and a display of turrets, cannon spouts, gablets and chimneys. The south front is perhaps the least satisfactory, bearing as it does a large triple window to the great hall inserted in the 1870s and a rather fussy clock, placed on a screen wall between two chimneys. Entry is now by the restored Queen Anne wing, beside the original entrance which still preserves its yett.

The vaulted ground floor has kitchens, store and small prison. The high hall on the first floor is an imposing vaulted space with three stone bosses carved with Hamilton cinquefoils and Burnett holly leaves crowning the vault, while the famous Horn of the Leys, traditionally presented by Bruce in 1323, hangs over the fireplace.

Crathes Castle (no. 22): painted ceiling of the Green Lady's Room

*Crathes Castle (no. 22): painted
ceiling of the Muses' Room*

*Crathes Castle (no. 22): painted
ceiling of the Nine Nobles' Room*

Above the hall are four rooms of particular interest. Three retain their original late 16th century painted ceilings which, with wall hangings and the dim light given by cruisie lamps and the shuttered and leaded windows, create a true 16th century ambiance. In the Nine Nobles' Room (1599), heroes of the past (Hector, Caesar, Alexander, King David, Joshua, Judas Maccabeus, King Arthur, Charlemagne and Godfrey de Bouillon, the crusader) are painted in colourful, even fanciful versions–an all-blue Julius Caesar with broadsword and mitre–in the narrow spaces between the beams of the ceiling. The Green Lady's Room has grotesques and mottoes to add to its legendary ghost, while in the Muses' Room the colours, essentially green, are particularly sombre yet vibrant.

Some excellent furniture characteristic of the late 16th century Aberdeen school of woodworking can also be seen, including two fine chairs in the Nine Nobles' Room and a massive four-poster bed of 1594 in the Laird's Bedroom. The wooden ceiling of the spacious Long Gallery at the top of the house is also an important piece of carpentry.

Crathes Castle (no. 22): south front

Fyvie Castle (no. 23), from S

Finally, the eight gardens, set within yew hedges that go back to the early 18th century, are of exceptional appeal.

23* Fyvie Castle, Fyvie, Banff and Buchan

Mid 13th–late 19th centuries AD.
NJ 763393. 11 km S of Turriff, off B 9005 Fyvie/Ellon road.
NTS.

On first approaching Fyvie, the modern visitor may initially be slightly disappointed, arriving as he does in the angle of two lofty wings and confronted with an evidently late, single-storey vestibule, with, to one side, a towering, keep-like structure complete with late Victorian heraldic frontispiece. The composition is unbalanced and the visitor confused.

In understanding Fyvie, the key insight is that it began life as a 13th century quadrangular castle of enclosure, a great square of c 50 m enclosed by a massive curtain wall 2.5 m thick with projecting towers at the corners. Therefore, the visitor standing before William Gordon's vestibule is already in the very centre of the ancient structure, having passed over the now levelled north and east walls.

This becomes clearer on the prospect of the famous south front or 'show facade'. While the upper work on the 50 m long front represents one of the finest

Fyvie Castle (no. 23): the great staircase

1500 by the Meldrums, who created the palace-like layout of chambers on the first floor of the west wing (the hall, outer chamber, and inner chamber, now the drawing-room, small drawing-room and charter room). In 1596 the castle was sold to Alexander Seton, first earl of Dunfermline and Chancellor of Scotland. He was probably responsible for the elaborate upper works. He certainly created the noble staircase, 4 m wide, leading to the main apartments; modelled on the staircase at Chaumont, Fyvie's stair is one of the most impressive of any date in Scotland. His grandson, the fourth earl, around 1686, inserted the door and dramatic red ashlar centrepiece on the south front.

Much was to change as a result of the Jacobite sympathies of the fourth earl. Exiled, his estates were confiscated and passed into Gordon hands. From 1770 to 1840 General William Gordon and his son carried out sweeping changes, the most dramatic being the demolition of the north and east wings, the building of the new vestibule and the Gordon Tower. This last, at the north end of the west wing, was built to provide more spacious chambers such as a ballroom; it blends remarkably well with the earlier work. The policies were also radically improved.

In 1889 the castle was purchased by Alexander Forbes-Leith, a local man who had amassed a fortune in America. With the Gordon alterations and the Forbes-Leith refurbishment, which included the Leith Tower, the original interior work was mostly removed. There is good late 16th century woodwork in the Charter Room and in the small chamber at the head of the great stairs. Otherwise, interest in the interior focuses on the fine paintings (including more than 12 outstanding Raeburns) and furniture which offer a diverting history of taste; all excellently presented by the Trust.

The influence of the later lairds of Fyvie is seen vividly in the parish kirk, described in the introduction to the next chapter.

flowerings of Scottish baronial architecture, the basic structure of projecting angle towers, wing walls and central gatehouse tower with drums is wholly medieval in conception.

Briefly, the early curtain wall, now embedded in the south and west fronts, may have been built in the early 13th century when Fyvie was the *caput* of the Thanage of Formartine. It remained in royal hands until 1380; 10 years later it passed to Sir Henry Preston who heightened the walls and rebuilt the corner towers. The castle was further enlarged between 1440 and

24 Glenbuchat Castle, Strathdon, Gordon

Late 16th century AD.
NJ 397148. 18 km W of Alford, off A 97 Huntly/
Ballater road.
HBM(SDD).

A no-nonsense Z-plan castle, Glenbuchat stands, foursquare above the ravine of the Water of Buchat. Built in 1590 by John Gordon and Helen Carnegie, whose initials can still be seen on the door lintel, the exterior is restrained, the three large offset blocks rising to corbelled square caphouses and crowsteps, giving it an angular look.

A French origin has been claimed for the two arches or *trompes* in the angles on the northern face, but they are as likely to have been inspired by local medieval squinch arches. The walls, which would have been harled, are pierced by many gun-loops, including one covering the door from the turret above.

The first floor of the main block contains the great hall, with laird's chamber in the north-east tower. Extensive alterations included the partitioning of the hall and the reworking of the upper floors (hence the odd four-light window on the west gable).

In all this is a building of solid grace still within the dictates of defence.

Glenbuchat Castle (no. 24)

Corgarff Castle (no. 25)

25* Corgarff Castle, Cockbridge, Gordon

Mid 16th and mid 18th centuries AD.
NJ 254086. 17 km N of Ballater, off A 939
Ballater/Tomintoul road.
HBM(SDD).

Standing high and lonely, in command of the road-links to the Dee, the Avon and the Don, Corgarff's plain white walls belie a turbulent history. The oblong tower at the core of the structure was built in 1537 but damaged in 1571 when a party of Gordons from Auchindoun Castle burned the castle, along with the laird's wife, Margaret Forbes, her family and servants 'to a total of 27'. This foul deed, part of the endemic Gordon/Forbes, Catholic/Protestant rivalry, is told in the ballad *Edom o' Gordon*.

In 1645 Montrose spent a month here before the battle of Alford and in 1715 the earl of Mar encamped here before raising the Jacobite standard at Braemar.

The most striking feature of Corgarff, the star-shaped curtain wall, was built in 1748 when, like Braemar Castle (NO 156923), it was taken over by the Hanoverian government and garrisoned as a centre from which to track down Jacobite rebels. The curtain wall is pierced by musket loops, while the two single-storey pavilions that flank the tower were also added then as bakehouse/brewhouse (west) and guardroom and prison (east).

The final episode in the castle's life came in 1827-31 when a captain, subaltern and 56 men were stationed here to check the whisky smuggling in Strathdon. The tower has now been restored and the barrack room furnished with double box-beds and cast-iron fuel boxes and grates.

26* Tolquhon Castle, Tarves, Gordon

Early 15th and late 16th centuries AD.
NJ 872286. 8 km E of Oldmeldrum, off B 999
Aberdeen/Tarves road.
HBM(SDD).

Tolquhon Castle (no. 26): William Forbes's south range

At Tolquhon a spacious, confident solution to the changed accommodation needs of a Renaissance laird can be seen. By 1584 the dour confines of the medieval Preston Tower, built in 1420 with walls 3 m thick, no longer provided an adequate standard of accommodation for the cultured laird, William Forbes. In that year he embarked on a radical 'new wark' (commemorated on a tablet to the right of the gatehouse), consisting of four ranges set round an open courtyard.

That this was the building of a new, Renaissance man is seen first in the gatehouse which, with its thin walls, large windows and fanciful gun loops, is more a vehicle for displaying the Forbes and royal arms and a series of engaging sculptured figures than a serious defensive structure. The ranges that flank the inner courtyard were spacious and well appointed. The east range, incorporating the old tower, is the most ruinous; the south range, opposite the gatehouse, is a noble structure, once harled, with a little drum stair-tower bearing on the north-west skew stone the initials of the mason, Thomas Leiper. The ground floor of this range contains extensive service quarters, including an interesting servery in the drum; above were the hall and private chamber of the laird. The first floor of the west and south ranges consists of a most elegant gallery, in which the laird would have kept his books, and retiring rooms for conversation. The furnishings must be imagined from the inventory of 1589—books, tapestries, panelling, artillery and furniture.

The grounds of the castle were not neglected, a pleasance being laid out on the west and south sides, while 12 bee-boles can still be seen in the forecourt wall.

William Forbes died soon after his 'new wark' was completed. His tomb can still be seen in Tarves kirkyard (no. 43), a fine memorial to the creator of Tolquhon.

27* Huntly Castle, Huntly, Gordon

Late 12th-early 17th centuries AD.
NJ 532407. 0.8 km N of centre of Huntly.
HBM(SDD).

Three castles have guarded the crossing of the Deveron at its confluence with the Bogie. The first, the Peel of Strathbogie, was an earth and timber motte and bailey castle built in the late 12th century; the motte can still be seen. The second, built c 1400 on the bailey of the first castle, was a strong L-plan stone tower of the Gordons whose foundations can still be traced. The third, the Palace that rears up 20 m or more, was begun in the mid 15th century, remodelled in the 1550s and adorned with oriels and armorials in the early 17th century.

Huntly features prominently in Scottish history. Sir Robert Bruce rested in the motte in 1307. James IV attended the marriage of the pretender to the English throne, Perkin Warbeck, to Lady Catherine Gordon in 1496 in the third castle. In 1556 the Queen Regent, Mary of Guise, visited this, the chief stronghold of the Catholic Gordon earls of Huntly that by 1562 was to become the headquarters of the counter reformation in Scotland. In that year, after the earl of Huntly's defeat at Corrichie, at the hands of Mary Queen of Scots, the castle was pillaged, the contents including the treasures of St Machar's Cathedral, Aberdeen. In the troubles of the 17th century the castle was occupied by the Covenanters (in 1640) and in 1647 the 'Irish' garrison was hanged, their officers beheaded, the marquis of Huntly captured and his escort shot against the walls.

The Palace is best preserved. It is of three periods, the earliest, dating to the mid 15th century, is represented by three basement vaults and a dark pit-prison cut into the foundations. Early graffiti survive on the plaster of the corridor. In the middle of the 16th century the fourth earl rebuilt this castle from the ground floor up. On the first floor is the earl's apartment, the traditional arrangement of hall, great chamber and inner chamber with bed recess and privy. The imagination must supply the wall hangings, window glass, plastered walls and painted ceilings (with 'figures and mottoes') with which these apartments would have been furnished.

The arrangement of the floor above, for the earl's wife, would have been similar. In the upper hall is one of the splendid heraldic mantelpieces inserted by George, first marquis, in the third building period, the first

Baronial splendour: Huntly Castle (no. 27)

decade of the 17th century. This shows the arms of Huntly and Lennox with the royal arms above, and between obelisks bearing Seton crescents and Lennox fleurs de lis. The topmost panel was removed by the Covenanter, Capt James Wallace as it was of a sacred subject.

At the top of the round tower, 20 m up, a 'belvedere' or turrret room gave wide, dizzying views. The first marquis also added the impressive heraldic frontispiece over the main doorway, to one Lord Lyon 'probably the most splendid heraldic doorway in the British Isles'. (It is fully explained in the site guidebook.) The gracious oriel windows on the south front were probably inspired by Huntly's visit to Blois in France in 1594. With the frieze of giant relief letters commemorating himself (GEORGE GORDOVN FIRST MARQVIS OF HVNTLIE) and his wife (HENRIETTE STEVART MARQVESSE OF HVNTLIE) in 1602, they complete one of the most sophisticated buildings of its day. From the depths of its hopeless pit to the airy sweetness of its oriels it was always a statement of Gordon power.

Dunnottar Castle (no. 28): the Earl Marischal's keep

28* Dunnottar Castle, Stonehaven, Kincardine and Deeside

Late 14th-mid 17th centuries AD.
NO 881838. 1.5 km S of Stonehaven, off A 92 Stonehaven/Montrose road.

The sheer cliffs of conglomerate that form the natural defences of this spectacular site define an area so large (3.5 ha) that successive occupiers have been able to develop a castle layout that is almost unique. The earliest use of the site is obscure; it may have been the *Dun Fother* of the early annals.

Today, the visitor climbs to the only entrance, the door through the 9 m high curtain, under the gaunt shadow of the five-storey height of the 16th century Benholm's Lodging. Once through the curtain and portcullis, the approach is still upwards, past the 16th century guardroom and magazine, along a steeply enclosed roadway and through two (8 m long) vaulted pends until one finally emerges on the grass platform of the interior. Around is almost a small town of buildings of varying dates.

The earliest extant structure is round to the right, in the most easily defended south-western corner of the plateau, the late 14th century L-plan keep. This imposing tower, 15 m high, was built by Sir William

Dunnottar Castle (no. 28): the Quadrangle

Keith, Great Marischal of Scotland, and extended in the 16th century.

The range of roofless buildings runnning east from the keep comprises storehouse, smithy and stables of the 16th century. North of the stables is the Priest's House or Waterton's Lodging, a 16th century free-standing house of two storeys.

Further east, occupying the north-eastern quarter of the plateau, is the great Quadrangle or 'Palace', measuring 45.8 m by 40.2 m. This group of buildings comprises a complete mansion house, spread out round a courtyard in a most un-Scottish plan. That it is almost unique is the result of its cliff-girt location which permitted a spaciousness of layout unknown elsewhere. The west range is the earliest part, having been built in the last quarter of the 16th century, and consists of seven chambers or 'lodgings' for guests or retainers. Each lodging has its own front door and

fireplace on the ground floor; a long gallery runs the whole length of the first floor of this range. The great hall is in the north range, built in the first half of the 17th century, with the lord's private chambers adjacent, in the wing projecting from the north-east corner over the Whigs' Vault of 1645. The east range has private bedrooms over brewery and bakehouse, while the south side of the quadrangle is completed by the 16th century chapel (which has earlier fragments incorporated in the fabric).

The history of Dunnottar is naturally one of siege and drama. Two events stand out, both from the 17th century. First the saving of the Honours of Scotland from Cromwell's grasp in 1652, by lowering them over the cliff and hiding them in Kinneff Kirk (no. 39). Second the imprisonment and ill usage of 122 men and 45 women Covenanters in 1685 in the Whigs' Vault–'the event whose dark shadow is for evermore flung athwart the Castled Rock'.

29* Balvenie Castle, Dufftown, Moray

Late 13th-late 16th centuries AD.
NJ 326408. 0.9 km N of the centre of Dufftown, turn E off A 941 Dufftown/Craigellachie road. HBM(SDD).

This is probably the Comyn castle of Mortlach which was already in existence by 1304. Commanding the mouths of Glen Rinnes and Glen Fiddich, the passes to Huntly, Keith and Cullen and the route to Elgin, it is perched on a promontory high above the River Fiddich.

Much of the form of the early castle of enclosure (45.7 m by 39.6 m) can still be seen. The great quadrangular curtain wall (2.1 m thick and from 7.6 m to 10.7 m tall) still stands grey and gritty, although the projecting angle towers have gone. The immense, vertically sided ditch still lies on the south and west. The hall and great chamber would have been on the west side of the courtyard. In the 15th century the kitchen was against the south wall, and its great flue can still be traced, as can the brew cauldron-setting in the brew house.

The early 16th century saw the building of a range of service chambers against the inside of the east wall; the northern half of this range was rebuilt between 1547 and 1557 by John Stewart the fourth earl of Atholl. The three building periods can be seen clearly on the east entrance front. The Atholl building with large round tower and moulded windows is rather more of a domestic structure. The three armorial panels are the royal arms, Atholl's own arms and those of his wife Lady Elizabeth Gordon. The family motto is displayed on a long scroll beneath the earl's arms: 'forth fortune and fill thy coffers'. The interior face of the Atholl building is no less imposing, with two tall stair drums, the northern being neatly corbelled out to the square, terminating in a crowstepped gable. These gave access to the new principal apartments, the hall and the outer and inner chambers (this last in the great corner tower, as at Huntly, no. 27).

Balvenie Castle (no. 29): the east range

Balvenie Castle (no. 29): east range from the courtyard

30* Kildrummy Castle, Alford, Gordon

13th century AD.
NJ 454163. 12 km W of Alford on the Huntly/
Ballater road (A 97).
HBM(SDD).

One of the few great stone castles of enclosure to have survived in Scotland from the high point of medieval European castle building, Kildrummy's broken grey walls lie like giant shattered eggshells. Defended to the north by the steep natural den, from which the stone for the castle was quarried, and with a broad ditch dug on the other sides, in plan Kildrummy is shield-shaped (with the flat top to the north).

It appears that the castle as first constructed in the early 13th century for Alexander II was a plain polygonal enclosure; this phase is represented by the coursed rubble of the east, west and south curtains. In the middle of the century the chapel was constructed and, to achieve a true east-west axis, was allowed to breach the curtain (in a manner 'that defies rational and learned explanation'). Subsequently, possibly as a result of the visit of Edward I of England in 1296, the towers, the ashlar plinth of the north curtain and the gatehouse were added, to produce a castle with remarkable similarities to the Edwardian castles of Harlech and Caernarvon, and, closer to Grampian, Bothwell in Strathclyde.

Important early features of the interior include the archers' slits and prison in the Warden's tower (in the north-east), the adjacent postern gate and portcullis, the great hall against the north curtain, and the great donjon or Snow Tower in the north-west which follows early French models. Later refashioning of the castle included the Elphinstone tower, a 16th century tower-house at the west end of the hall and the bakehouse complex in the south-east.

The castle saw many sieges, notably in 1306 when Sir Nigel Bruce (King Robert's brother) held it against the young Prince Edward of Caernarvon until betrayed by Osbarn the smith (who was rewarded, it is said, by having the gold he had been promised poured molten down his throat). The castle was restored (most evident in west curtain), besieged in 1335 by Balliol forces, burnt in 1530, captured by Cromwell in 1654, and became the headquarters of the Earl of Mar's Jacobite rising of 1715, after which it was dismantled.

Kildrummy Castle (no. 30): the Warden's Tower

Kildrummy Castle (no. 30): the great castle of enclosure from SW

31* Drum Castle, Drumoak, Kincardine and Deeside

Late 13th-17th centuries AD.
NJ 796005. 16 km W of Aberdeen, N off A 93 Aberdeen/Banchory road.
NTS.

Of the many baronial residences of various dates that are to be seen in Grampian, the progenitor may be said to be the mighty Tower of Drum. Seven centuries old, with red granite walls 3.7 m thick, it rises 21.5 m to its corbelled wall-walk and deep crenellations. In plan it is a simple rectangle, 16.2 m by 11.9 m, with rounded corners.

It may have been built initially as a royal fortress, commanding the old road running north into the province of Mar from the Cryne Corse Mounth and the ford of Dee at the Mills of Drum. In 1323 king Robert gave the Forest of Drum to his armour-bearer William de Irwin; from then until 1976 the castle was in Irvine hands.

The original, first-floor entrance to the Tower survives, but not the protective barmkin that must have surrounded it. The Laigh Hall on the first floor was converted to a library in the 19th century and is now entered from the 17th century house. (It is still possible to appreciate the soaring medieval

Medieval strength: the great Tower of Drum (no. 31)

The old wood of Drum

proportions of this room despite the distractions of the heraldic decoration of the vault and the bizarre Angel Gabriel self-portrait by Hugh Irvine.)

For a truly medieval experience, however, the visitor should climb the worn turnpike stair from the original Tower entrance to the vast pointed barrel-vaulted cavity above the Laigh Hall. Here, with the timber floor of the third storey now gone (but its strong corbels still evident) the traveller can sit on a seven hundred year-old seat by a square open window within the bare, massive walls. In this dim light he can explore the garderobe in the north-west corner, whose channel falls 7.6 m down through the wall.

The parapet walk and high merlons at the top of the Tower are uniquely well preserved, although the original tall caphouse has gone. From here one can see the later additions to Drum, principally the mansion house of c 1619. Apart from its notable formal rooms, the lesser quarters are particularly fine, consisting principally the basement kitchen and dairy, which are ranged off a striking stone-flagged corridor that runs the full length of the building. Above stairs, the Green Closet, overlooking the front door, with its 18th century panelling and furniture of a practical elegance preserves much of the feel of life in the times of improvement.

An important additional feature of Drum, one that links back beyond even the days of the Tower, is the fragment of the Old Wood that survives on the property. The enormous oaks and pines that stand at random and the gnarled geans (wild cherry trees) mingling with them are a remnant of the native Caledonian Forest that once cloaked most of the north-east. Something of the primeval atmosphere of that great forest can be gained from a walk in the Old Wood of Drum.

32 Duffus Castle, Duffus, Moray

Mid 12th and late 13th centuries AD.
NJ 189672. 6 km NW of Elgin, on side road E of
B 9102 Elgin/Hopeman road.
HBM(SDD).

The essentially alien nature of the motte and bailey
castles erected as part of Norman feudalism can be
appreciated at Duffus. Out of the now fertile but then
swampy Laich rises a green but windswept mound
topped by a broken stone castle.

The castle that David I stayed in when inspecting the
building work at his new foundation, Kinloss Abbey,
in 1151, would have been a timber tower surrounded
by a stockade, set on the artificial mound. The deep
defensive ditch that separated the motte from the
bailey can still be seen.

The stone castle that now crowns the motte may have
been the one damaged by the Moray uprising of 1297
during the Wars of Independence. It is an unusual
stone keep with timber floors of 11 m span, supported
on piers.

In the event, the weight of the huge tower proved too
much for the gravel mound; the collapsed masonry of
the north-west corner sprawls, still bonded, on the
motte side. The bailey is surrounded by the footings of
a curtain wall with a 15th century domestic range of
hall and cellars against its north inner face; the latter
have been built over the motte ditch into which they
have partially collapsed. Around the whole
fortification is a boundary ditch, now water-filled,
enclosing c 3.2 ha.

Duffus Castle (no. 32): motte and bailey

Duffus Castle (no. 32): the motte and the keep from the bailey

33 Peel of Lumphanan, Lumphanan, Kincardine and Deeside

13th century AD.
NJ 576036. 1 km SW of Lumphanan, on side road off A 980 Banchory/Alford road.
HBM(SDD).

One of Grampian's earliest medieval earthworks, this flat-topped mound, 36.6 m by 45.7 m, rises 9 m above an enclosing ditch, 15 m wide, itself retained by an earthen bank. Formerly interpreted as a shell-keep, a motte with a curtain wall, excavations in the 1970s established that the wall around the summit was a late 18th century dyke built by the usual 'zealous agriculturalists'. The original 13th century defences may have been a turf rampart rather than a palisade. The motte was built by the Durwards.

The footings of a rectangular manor house, Halton House, on the mound summit, date from the late 15th century. The original cobbled causeway was traced across the ditch and winding up the north-east side of the motte. The water in the wide ditch may have been controlled by a sluice system, now vanished.

The Doune of Invernochty (no. 34)

34 Doune of Invernochty, Strathdon, Gordon

Late 12th/early 13th century AD.
NJ 351129. 25 km W of Alford on B 973 at Strathdon.

This is a massive Norman castle earthwork, the 'capital messuage' of Strathdon, one of the feudal lordships of the province of Mar. Carved out of a glacial mound, the motte is oval in plan and measures an enormous 76 m by 36.6 m and 18.3 m in height. It is surrounded by a ditch and bank. Only two other Norman earthworks are of comparable size, the Motte of Urr in Kirkcudbrightshire and Duffus castle in Moray (no. 32).

The scale (1.8 m thick) and mortaring of the curtain wall around the summit suggest that it is a genuine military work rather than a late dyke as at Lumphanan (no. 33). The oblong building whose foundations stretch right across the summit may have been a chapel, in view of the rare carved piscina or stoup fragment found close by; this building may have served as the parish church of Invernochty until later medieval times. The square foundations near the entrance on the south side of the summit may have been a tower.

The motte is surrounded by a broad ditch which could be flooded from a lake immediately to the west, whose eastern retaining bank can still be seen running through the trees. This, and the sluices that controlled the water at the north-west and east of the counter-scarp, represent an important and rare example of early military engineering.

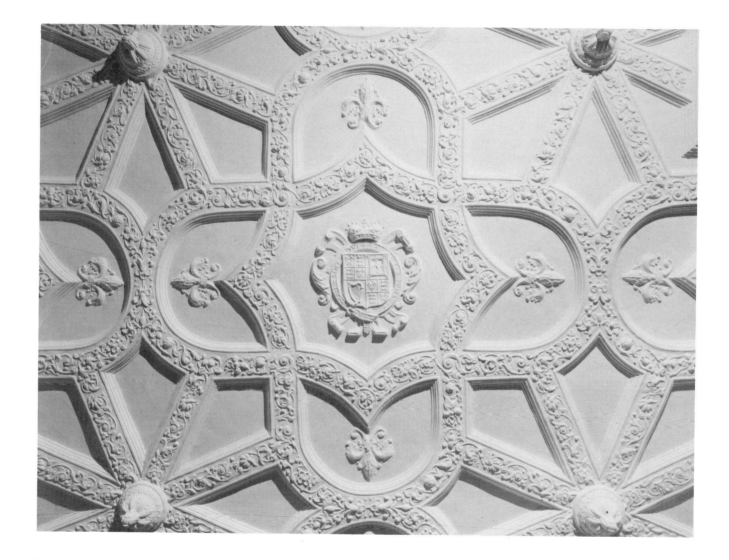

Craigievar Castle (no. 20): detail of plaster ceiling in bedroom on third floor.

4

PRELATES AND PRESBYTERIES

As a potent force in the area for over 1000 years, Christianity has left a rich and varied legacy of buildings, ruins and monuments. Owing largely to the effects of time, the indifference of the early reformed church to its inheritance of buildings and the schismatic tendencies of the Presbyterians of the 18th and 19th centuries, the bulk of the material is late in date.

Some post-Reformation kirks have interesting historical associations (eg Kinneff, no. 39, or Crathie, no. 35). Others are typical of the Scottish reformed kirk of the 18th and 19th centuries (ie after the Presbyterian settlement of 1689), where the preaching of the word, rather than the administering of the sacrament, was of paramount importance. This had been emphasised from early in the Reformation, for in 1596 the kirk of St Nicholas in Aberdeen was divided by a wall at the crossing to create 'ane preaching Kirk' from the choir. The later churches of Longside (no. 36), with its three-sided gallery focused on the pulpit, or Edinkillie (no. 38), with its central pulpit, are very different in scale but were specifically built for this purpose. This emphasis on the Word is perhaps seen most literally in the great three-decker pulpit at Dyke kirk (NH 990584). Although many visitors may find such churches plain to the point of austerity, the best country kirks of this period (eg Spynie, Quarrywood, NJ 182642; Botriphnie, NJ 375441; Kildrummy, no. 37; or Glass, NJ 434399) have a quiet simplicity that is seemly and utterly Scots.

The rare calm of Pluscarden Abbey (no. 46)

Many of these kirks were built on the site of earlier churches and therefore stand within kirkyards of considerable antiquity. The kirkyards of Grampian provide a wealth of interest, whether for an excellent range of inscribed gravestones and figure monuments, as at Bellie (no. 42), St Peter's, Duffus (no. 51), Cullen (no. 50), Tarves (no. 43), Kildrummy (no. 37), Marnoch (NJ 593499), Fyvie (NJ 768377), St Mary's, Banff (NJ 690640), or Fordyce (NJ 555638), or for individual features of historical interest, eg the memorial to the Protestant martyr George Wishart at Auchenblae (NO 725784), the Covenanters' stone in Dunnottar kirkyard, said to have inspired Scott's *Old Mortality* (NO 863852), the stone at Kinkell (no. 52) of Gilbert de Greenlaw who fell at Harlaw in 1411, or even the grave of John Brown at Crathie old kirk (NO 264947).

Many of these now tranquil kirkyards contain echoes of a noisier past. Markets were often held in kirkyards, as the mercat crosses that survive at St Peter's, Duffus (no. 51), Dallas kirk (NJ 121518), and Kineddar (NJ 223695) testify; there was a popular market in the kirkyard of Kincardine O'Neil (NO 592996) as it was located close to one of the important crossings of the Dee. The growth of medical education at the end of the 18th century created a demand for fresh corpses for study which led to the activities of the resurrectionists or body snatchers. Many of the region's kirkyards still contain little watch-towers (eg Mortlach, no. 56; St Machar's, no. 48; Edinkillie, no. 38; Marnoch, NJ 593499; St Fergus, NK 115507), from

which a new grave could be guarded, often by 'watch societies'. A few kirkyards also preserve ingenious mortsafes (eg Cluny, no. 41; Tough, NJ 615129; Towie, NJ 439129) or vaults (eg Udny, no. 40; Fintray, NJ 840165; Kemnay, NJ 737160).

In Grampian, the churches themselves, of all denominations, often contain stained glass of Victorian or more recent date, some of which repays study. St Laurence's, Forres (NJ 035588), Crathie Kirk (no. 35), the chapels at Haddo House (no. 3) and Drum Castle (no. 31), the kirk of Arbuthnott (no. 53) and St Drostan's Episcopal church, Old Deer (NJ 978476) all have fine later 19th century windows. Excellent 20th century glass is to be seen at Fyvie Kirk (NJ 768377) where there are two Tiffany windows, quite out of place but totally ravishing; St Machar's Aberdeen (no. 48), particularly the east window of 1953; and at Pluscarden Abbey (no. 46) where the community now manufactures its own magnificent glass. Finally, a number of windows incorporate local landscapes or objects, such as Strachan's impressive Bishop's window in St Machar's (no. 48), the windows on the south side of Mortlach Kirk (no. 56), and in Monymusk (no. 55) and Birnie (no. 57) kirks. These

last three all include depictions of the Pictish stones that have been found nearby.

Such sites with Pictish stones (to which should be added Tullich, NO 390975; Deer, NJ 979476; and Fordoun, NO 726784) were certainly early centres of the faith; they also emphasise, however, how little is known of the origins of Christianity in Grampian. Although notes added in the 12th century to the ninth century gospels, the *Book of Deer*, record the tradition that Columba and Drostan came from Iona to Aberdour (ie in the mid sixth century), where they received two grants of land from the Pictish *mormaer*, Bede, it is not until the seventh century that definite evidence for Christian foundations is known. These were at Aberdour, west of Fraserburgh, and Forglen, near Turriff. The latter, interestingly, was the church where the *breacbannoch* or shrine containing a relic of St Columba (later carried before the Scottish host at Bannockburn) and known subsequently as the Monymusk Reliquary, was housed. (It is now in the Royal Museum of Scotland.) Deer, in Buchan, Tullich and Aboyne on Deeside, Mortlach in upper Moray, Birnie near Elgin, Monymusk on the Don, Forvie on the Ythan and Fordoun in the Mearns were all sites of

Christian activity during the later first millennium AD. Many are now associated with Pictish symbol stones, although the precise relationship of the early stones with Christianity is still unclear; they are discussed in the next chapter.

The central event in the history of the Scottish kirk was, of course, the Reformation of the mid 16th century. Two aspects of this change can be seen in Grampian. The first, which was more evident in the north-east than elsewhere in Scotland, was the measure of toleration accorded to Catholics (and, later, to Episcopalians). The second, which was more universal, was the degree of patronage exercised by powerful individuals and groups both before and after the Reformation.

Monymusk Reliquary, the breacbannoch of St Columba

The fine churches in Huntly, Buckie and Keith and the cathedral in Aberdeen are the modern face of Roman Catholicism in Grampian. The survival of a body of practising Catholics after the Reformation is explained by a number of factors. First, the major Catholic nobleman in Scotland was the Gordon earl of Huntly; the Catholic enclave on the Braes of Enzie that sheltered Thomas Nicholson, from 1697 the first Vicar Apostolic, was very much in Gordon country. Second, the remoteness of much of the region helped small foundations like the college at Scalan on the Braes of Glenlivet (NJ 246194) to survive (although it was burned during the intensification of persecution following the 'Forty-five'). Third, and most important, the wilder excesses of the Reformers had never been popular in the north-east. In Aberdeen itself, for example, both the Reformation of 1560 and the Covenant of 1638 had to be imposed by force. Even so, the last Catholic Bishop of Aberdeen remained in his palace, enjoying most of his revenues, until his death in 1577. That the church of James VI, which was Calvinist in doctrine but hierarchical in structure, was greatly liked in the north-east may be explained by a form of 'innate conservatism', yet it was surely more than this that led the Aberdeen Doctors, alone of Scottish 17th century academics, to see the extreme Presbyterians as standing in the way of a united, if reformed, church.

Turning to the theme of lay patronage, which has been an essential element in church architecture, its origins were royal or noble, as in David I's foundation of Kinloss Abbey (NJ 065615) or William, first Comyn earl of Buchan's grant to the Abbey of Deer (NJ 968481) in 1219. By the end of the medieval period, lesser gentry were making endowments, for example, the aisle at Arbuthnott (no. 53), the collegiate church at Cullen (no. 50) or the sacrament house at Deskford (no. 49). Such gifts were to glorify god, although it is assumed that some honour reflected on the donor.

A late medieval church interior:
Greyfriars Convent of Mercy, Elgin

The Reformers initially discouraged any such gifts, and attempted to rid the churches of images and craftsmanship thought to be idolatrous: the 'substantious and honourable' choir stalls and organ of St Nicholas, Aberdeen, were sawn up in 1574. During the 17th century, however, a different kind of church furnishing began to be permitted—elaborately carved pews or lofts for the use of the lairds or trade guilds. The laird's loft of 1634 in Pitsligo church (NJ 934662) is a particularly ornate example. In 1642 the great reredos of St Machar's was taken down by order of the Presbytery and the wood used to build a 'beistlie loft' across the west end. The apogee of this curious reversal that the reformed church permitted, the glorification of post-Reformation man as distinct from the exaltation of pre-Reformation God, is surely the extraordinary 'pew' created for the Lord Provost of Aberdeen in 1751 in West St Nicholas, a 'pedimented and baldichinoed conceit' placed in the centre of the east end of the church. The influence of the lairds and other heritors continued into the 19th century and can be seen in the late 'Castle loft' at Fyvie, the memorial tablets in Monymusk (no. 54) and the fittings of Crathie (no. 35).

Finally, a preference which may stem ultimately from the blind zeal of the early Reformers and which continues to mar some of our best medieval churches is the taste for bare, unrendered interior walls. The exposure of rubble that the medieval builder never intended to be shown is a tradition dear to many congregations. In St Machar's Cathedral, the major feature, the ceiling, is isolated from the rest of the building by bare clerestorey walls. By contrast, the sensitive restoration of the late 15th century convent church of Greyfriars, Elgin (NJ 219627), with walls decently clad, provides the closest approximation to a functioning medieval church in the north-east.

Crathie Kirk (no. 35)

Longside Kirk (no. 36)

35 Crathie Kirk, Crathie and Braemar, Kincardine and Deeside

AD 1893-5.
NO 265949. 9 km W of Ballater. Park in public carpark beside A 93.

Perched on a ledge above the Dee, this tall cruciform church is the work of A Marshall Mackenzie; it replaces a church of 1804. From the west door, the first impression of the interior is deceptively simple: a rather dull kirk with bare grey walls, dark woodwork and high, bright windows. On approaching the crossing, Mackenzie's skill becomes evident. He has contrived a space of generalised ecclesiastical intent (nodding to several different traditions), which can function as a place of public worship for the Royal Family when at Balmoral. The royal pew is in the south transept, entered from a wooden porch. The wide, shallow chancel is decidedly Anglican in inspiration, being approached up four steps and containing a grandiose marble 'communion table' (equalled in the Scottish Kirk only in the metropolitan splendour of St Cuthbert's, Edinburgh) and a hexagonal pulpit that is also a minor lapidarium (fashioned from 18 different granites and bearing pebbles of Iona marble collected by HRH Princess Louise). Crathie's secondary, and compelling, function as a royal ancestor shrine is seen most clearly in the central space, the crossing, whose pillars contain canopied recesses for portrait busts of Queen Victoria, King George V and King George VI.

36 Longside Parish Church, Longside, Banff and Buchan

AD 1835-6.
NK 037472. In Longside village, 10 km W of Peterhead.

The old kirk of 1620, its gateway, the tombstones and the new kirk form an interesting and characteristic group. Entered through an unusual gateway of 1620, resembling a lychgate, with a 1705 finial, the old parish kirk is a roofless rectangle with a fine birdcage bellcote with cornice.

The new kirk that was built by the Aberdeen architect John Smith in 1835-6 is exceptionally large and functional; the exterior is unadorned but for a plain bellcote and a clock. Inside, there is seating for 1350 people, with a high, three-sided gallery focusing on the substantial pulpit that occupies the east wall. Here the preaching of the Presbyterian word was the supreme activity.

The kirkyard contains some good 18th century stones, the grave of the Episcopalian minister, John Skinner (author of *Tullochgorum* and other songs, and father of Bishop Skinner) and an obelisk marking the grave of Jamie Fleeman (the 'laird of Udny's fool') (1713-78).

37 Kildrummy Kirk, Kildrummy, Gordon
AD 1805.
NJ 472175. 11 km W of Alford, off A 97 Huntly/Ballater road.

This unusual, rectangular, bow-fronted church with central bellcote replaced, in 1805, the pre-Reformation church whose remains still stand on the green kirkyard mound behind. Within all is light and airy, the pulpit being placed between two large windows on the east, with a horseshoe-shaped gallery of light wood opposite. The font from the old kirk is here.

There is some doubt whether the grassy mound on which the old kirk of St Bride's sits was a motte, the precursor of the castle at Kildrummy (no. 30). An arched Gothic recess on the north wall, possibly an Easter sepulchre, contains a fine relief effigy slab to the fourth laird of Brux, c 1400, which was reused in the 16th century.

38 Edinkillie Kirk, Dunphail, Moray
AD 1741.
NJ 019465. 12 km S of Forres, on A 940 Forres/Grantown road.

This plain oblong kirk is typical of the country areas of Grampian. Harled and cream-washed, it has round-headed windows and a little belfry. Within it is almost severe, with the traditional post-Reformation arrangement of the pulpit in the centre of the south wall and the communion table in front. Three small lofts have been squeezed in.

In the kirkyard, against the south wall, is a six-sided watch-house.

Kildrummy Kirk (no. 37)

Edinkillie Kirk (no. 38)

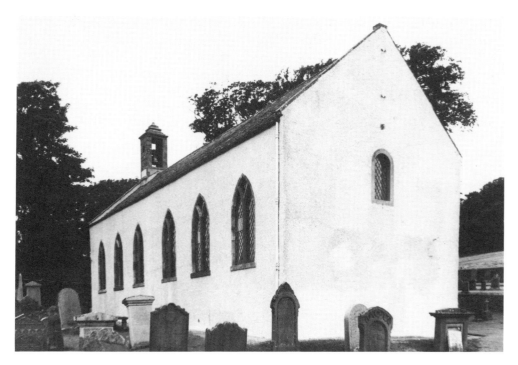

Kinneff old kirk (no. 39)

39 Kinneff Old Kirk, Inverbervie, Kincardine and Deeside

AD 1738.

NO 855748. 3 km NE of Inverbervie, on side road off A 92 Montrose/Stonehaven road.

An excellent example of a substantial T-plan Scottish kirk, it was largely rebuilt in 1738 and the north aisle added in 1876. The earlier church was most notable for having been the hiding place for the Honours of Scotland, the crown, sceptre and sword, that were smuggled out of Dunnottar Castle (no. 28) during Cromwell's seige of 1651. James Grainger, the minister, hid the crown and sceptre beneath a stone in front of the pulpit and the sword at the west end of the church; he and his wife dug up the Regalia at night once every three months in order to air them. Grainger's monument, with a suitably heroic inscription, is on the west wall. (There is also a memorial to the keeper of Dunnottar, George Ogilvie of Barras.)

Udny mort house (no. 40)

40 Udny Mort House, Udny Green, Gordon

AD 1832.

NJ 880262. 20 km N of Aberdeen, in graveyard on W side of green, on side road off B 999 Aberdeen/Tarves road.

This plain, circular building could be easily mistaken for a rather substantial toolstore. A second look at its solid granite masonry, its high, slated roof, the absence of windows, and its stout oak door reveals a most ingenious solution to the problem of the resurrectionists or body snatchers.

Coffins were placed within the mort house on a turntable, thus postponing burial until the bodies were unsuitable for sale. (Coffins were removed successively, the maximum period of storage being three months.) Four independent key-bearers were needed to unlock the oaken door and to penetrate the sliding inner iron door.

It was designed by Captain John Marr of Cairnbrogie and built for £80 Scots by Alexander Wallace and Thomas Smith in 1832, ironically the year of the passing of the *Anatomy (Scotland) Act* which ultimately solved the problem by ensuring an adequate legal supply of bodies.

The mort house was subsequently used as an ammunition store.

---

41   Cluny Old Kirkyard, Cluny, Gordon
18th/19th centuries AD.
NJ 684125. 13 km SW of Inverurie, on lane off side road (1 km SW of Kemnay) linking B 993 and A 944.

Cluny old kirkyard (no. 41): Miss Elyza Fraser's mausoleum and mortsafes

The old kirkyard rests on a little knoll opposite the present parish kirk of 1789. Its most striking feature is the splendid neo-classical mausoleum of 1808 to Miss Elyza Fraser of Castle Fraser (no. 21). Designed by her friend, the aesthete James Byers of Tonley (to whom she left her carriage and best pair of horses), it is of granite ashlar, circular in plan, sitting on a low plain square podium and rising to a tall, domed roof. The doorway is narrow and high, with an intricate wrought-iron grille, surmounted by a fine triangular heraldic panel. Around the frieze in elegant capitals is the inscription ELIZABETH FRASER OF CASTLE FRASER MDCCCVIII. It cost £353 and is the finest classical tomb in the north-east. In front of the mausoleum stand four mortsafes, consisting of iron cages which would have enclosed the coffin in the grave, topped by massive slabs of granite which would have been extremely difficult to shift clandestinely. Such weighty mortsafes required block and tackle to manoeuvre them into the grave; a set is preserved in Inverurie Museum.

42 Bellie Kirkyard, Fochabers, Moray

16th-20th centuries AD.
NJ 353610. 2 km N of Fochabers, on B 9104
Fochabers/Spey Bay road.

The old kirk of St Mary's (also dedicated to St Ninian) once stood where now an exceptionally varied range of gravestones climbs the gentle slope. The kirkyard is dominated by the classical temple mausoleum of 1825 to Jean Christie, second wife of the fourth duke of Gordon, and their children, consisting of twelve unfluted Ionic columns enclosing two small sarcophagi. Halfway down the slope is a slab of 1663 which records that William Saunders, who lived to 107, served as the first post-Reformation minister of the parish for an astounding 77 years. There are many fine 18th century table tombs (several with elegant palmettes carved on the supports), a particularly good series of rich Victorian uprights in sandstone, and a late (1920s) walltomb with bronze and marble portrait medallions. All human life is here, in death, from Indian nabobs to the teenage sisters, Isabella and Christina Maclean (d 1818) who were:

'Fortunate both in
having lived their short day
Strangers to the vices of the world
And departed ere it had fallen
to their lot to seek to regain
lost Happiness through the
Bitterness of Repentance'.

Bellie kirkyard (no. 42): the Gordon tomb

Bellie kirkyard (no. 42): detail of 18th century table tomb

105

43 Tolquhon Tomb, Tarves, Gordon
AD 1589.
NJ 869311. In kirkyard in Tarves, 25 km N of Aberdeen on B 999.
HBM (SDD).

In 1589, the creator of the 'new wark' at Tolquhon Castle (no. 43), the laird William Forbes, turned his mason, Thomas Leiper to the task of fashioning an elaborate tomb for himself and his wife. The tomb, which stood in the south aisle of the now vanish d kirk, is a richly decorated arched structure combining Gothic and Renaissance motifs. The overall scheme is medieval in character, but most of the detail echoes classical motifs, seen best on the flanking balusters. The arms and initials of William Forbes (d 1596) and his wife, Elizabeth Gordon, are in the upper corners of the tomb. The tracery is supported by little beruffed portrait statues of the couple. Several other stones in the kirkyard are of interest, particularly one of 1583 to the Craig family. The present kirk dates from 1798 and has good internal woodwork (horseshoe gallery, pews and a fine pulpit) of c 1825.

44* St Ninian's Church, Tynet, Moray
AD 1755.
NJ 378612. 4 km NE of Fochabers, N off A 98 Fochabers/Cullen road.

This unassuming white-harled rural building, which may be mistaken for a line of cottages, is the oldest building erected after the Reformation for Roman Catholic worship in Scotland. Built just nine years after Culloden, at a time when Catholics were regarded with suspicion if not direct hostility, this low building, in the Gordon lands of Enzie, was originally even more inconspicuous, having a thatched roof and no glazed windows. The ball finial on the west gable was added in 1779 by the priest George Matheson, who also glazed the windows and slated the roof. The interior is simple but pleasing.

The Tolquhon Tomb, Tarves (no. 43)

The inconspicuous St Ninian's, Tynet (no. 44)

45* St Gregory's Church, Preshome, Moray

AD 1788.

NJ 409614. 7 km NE of Fochabers, on side road 1 km E of Clochan.

Folded amongst the gentle Braes of Enzie, the Italian baroque west front of St Gregory's, Preshome, forms a triumphant contrast to the modest chapel at Tynet (no. 44). Built a generation after St Ninian's and within five years of the Catholic Relief bill, St Gregory's is obviously, even assertively, a church. The architect appears to have been the priest, Father John Reid, who was educated at the Scots College at Rome. In the west front he certainly contrived a remarkable composition, effectively doubling the width of the building by adding the staircase pavilions that flank the central doorpiece with its concave, unswept gable topped by a small pediment with urns and cross above. Lest there be any misapprehension, the inscription above the door reads simply 'DEO 1788'.

The grandiloquent St Gregory's, Preshome (no. 45)

46 Pluscarden Abbey, Elgin, Moray

13th century AD.

NJ 142576. 7 km SW of Elgin, on side road between Elgin and Rafford.

The Vale of Pluscarden, sheltering behind Heldon Hill, is a suitably serene location for that most rare of modern ecclesiastical sights, a working abbey. The simple crosses in the burial ground to the north-east of the abbey mark the graves of some of the modern monks who, since 1948, have gradually restored this great 13th century church.

Founded by Alexander II in 1230, Pluscarden was one of only three Valliscaulian priories in Scotland or England which were daughters of the Priory of Val des Choux in Burgundy. (The others were Beauly in Highland Region and Ardchattan in Strathclyde Region.) Pluscarden was dedicated to St Mary and St John, the two patrons of the order, and to St Andrew. In 1454 Pluscarden became a Benedictine house after union with the Priory of Urquhart, 7 km east of Elgin. After the Reformation, some monks remained for several decades.

The revival of the priory began with its purchase in 1897 by that remarkable Catholic antiquarian, John, third marquis of Bute, who proceeded with 'the conscientiousness of a traditionalist and the zeal of a convert' to repair parts of the building. In 1943 his son, Lord Colum Crichton-Stuart, presented the priory to the Benedictine community of Prinknash, near Gloucester, and in 1948 five of their monks began the work of restoration that is still continuing. (The restoration is to plans prepared by the distinguished Scottish architect and historian, Ian G Lindsay.) Raised to the status of an abbey in 1974, there are now nearly 30 monks, priests and novices.

The traveller enters the precincts through the original enclosure wall, one of the best preserved in the country, and approaches the east side of the restored

Pluscarden Abbey (no. 46), from SE

13th century AD.
NJ 221630. At E end of Elgin, signposted N off
A 96.
HBM (SDD).

'The noble and highly adored church of Moray', the
most beautiful of Scotland's medieval cathedrals.
Founded in 1224 as the seat of the bishopric of Moray
and dedicated to the Holy Trinity, work may have
begun on the great three-towered cathedral before the
see transferred from Spynie. The transepts, great,
boldly buttressed west towers and parts of the tall
choir and nave survive from the serious fire of 1270
that occasioned much rebuilding.

The reconstruction involved extending the presbytery
and adding aisles to the choir and to those already

church, with its simple tiered lancet windows, and the
range of pleasing conventual buildings (Chapter
House, Library, Refectory and Dormitory). The
tranquillity and beauty of the exterior are matched
inside. Entry is by a door in the north transept; it is
thought unlikely that the nave was ever completed.
The soft stone of the tall pillars of the crossing and the
old night-stair give back the blues and golds of the
great north rose window. There is now a fine tradition
of stained-glass manufacture at Pluscarden, seen most
spectacularly in the cataract of glorious reds and golds
that floods the restored chancel through the new east
lancets.

Around the chancel arch, repaired after the damage
traditionally ascribed to the Wolf of Badenoch in 1390,
are some unusual fragments of 15th century frescoes;
a seated St John can be seen on the north side.

The rare calm of Pluscarden remains long with the
traveller.

*Elgin Cathedral (no. 47): the
elongated presbytery and great east
end, from SE*

flanking the nave, thus producing an exceptionally wide nave, unique in Scotland. The south aisle had chapels, each with a separate gable; this feature, and the wide nave, were inspired by French examples. The octagonal chapter house was also built. The most notable feature that survives from this late 13th century rebuilding is the lofty presbytery which projects eastwards from the choir, beyond the line of the choir aisles, thus emphasising the high altar. This plan, the tiers of lancets in the east window (five on five, with a rose window above) and the rich corner octagonal towers are similar to St Andrew's Cathedral and Arbroath Abbey.

This great church stood until 1390, when Alexander Stewart, earl of Buchan and illegitimate son of Robert

The burning of Elgin Cathedral

II, in pursuit of his vendetta against the Bishop of Moray (Bishop Bur), who had excommunicated him for deserting his wife, burnt it and the towns of Elgin and Forres (and probably also Pluscarden Priory). The sacrilege and devastation caused by the Wolf of Badenoch required considerable rebuilding, although the 'books, charters and other valuables' that had perished could not be replaced. New windows were inserted in the choir aisles and the presbytery repaired almost immediately. Work continued throughout the 15th century and included the reconstruction (1482-1501) of the vault of the chapter house.

The treatment of the cathedral in post-Reformation times was lamentable. The lead was stripped from the roof by order of the Privy Council in 1567; the 'detestable bigot', Gilbert Ross, minister of Elgin, tore down the rood screen (with its 'starris of bricht golde') in 1640, and on Easter Sunday 1711 the great central tower fell, ruining the nave and transepts. The ruins were used as a 'common quarry' until 1807, when a wall was built round them. In 1816 they were taken under the control of the Barons of Exchequer who appointed John Shanks keeper in 1825. His tombstone in the graveyard records his labours of clearance and consolidation.

Many detached fragments of sculpture can be seen in the cathedral, notably an excellent bishop and a Pictish cross-slab (found in Elgin in 1823) with interlace-filled cross and possibly two evangelists on one face and a rectangular symbol, a double disc and Z-rod, a crescent and V-rod and a hunting scene on the other. There are also good table-tombs with heraldry in the surrounding graveyard.

Outside the cathedral, the so-called 'Bishop's House' is a substantial rectangular 16th century ruin, more correctly the manse of one of the cathedral canons (possibly the Precentor), while the fine gate through the precinct wall, the Pans Port, still survives to the east.

48 St Machar's Cathedral, Old Aberdeen, Aberdeen

14th/15th centuries AD.
NJ 939087. In Chanonry, off St Machar Drive in N Aberdeen.

As it stands today the great church of St Machar, on the curving River Don, represents half of the late medieval cathedral of the Bishops of Aberdeen. Probably the fourth church on this site, most of the fabric dates from the 15th century. The earliest surviving features are the western sandstone piers of

St Machar's Cathedral, Aberdeen (no. 48), from SW

the crossing which date from the late 14th century. However, the bulk of the surviving remains, principally the north transept and the militaristic west front, were built in granite by Bishop Henry Lichton between 1422 and 1440. In the early 16th century Bishop William Elphinstone rebuilt the choir and completed the central tower and Bishop Gavin Dunbar added the sandstone spires to the western towers and the transept, as well as commissioning the great ceiling.

Although now reduced to half its length (by the collapse of the central tower in 1688), St Machar's is still a most powerful creation. Severe, unadorned, as the use of granite at this early date dictated, it derives its considerable impact from the massing of the great western towers which rise to battlemented parapets carried on heavy, triple corbels. The tall angle buttresses and narrow ventilation slits add to the sense of strength. The steeples rise to a total height of 34 m from caphouses within the parapets. The great, military, bulk of these towers is relieved by the lancets that fill the west nave gable. Such a 'fortress church' is unique in Britain; east Germany and south-west France provide distant parallels.

The interior is also simple, if not austere, with plain drum columns forming eight bays with clerestorey and aisles. Its most notable feature is the heraldic timber ceiling, designed probably by Alexander Galloway, rector of Kinkell (no. 52) and executed by James Winter of Angus between 1519 and 1521, during the episcopate of Gavin Dunbar. The shields are arranged on the unusual, flat ceiling in three parallel rows with 16 shields in each row; the order of precedence descends from the east. In the southern row are the arms of the premier nobles of Scotland, headed by James V; the central row contains the arms of the Scottish prelates, headed by Pope Leo X, while the northern row has the sovereigns of Europe behind the emperor Charles V. It is likely that the ceiling was orientated on a statue of the Virgin and Child that stood (until 1640) above the west arch of the crossing, facing west down the nave. An important detail is that the arms of the king of Scots are surmounted by an enclosed crown similar to that of the holy Roman emperor, signifying a monarch with full jurisdiction within his realm. The ceiling may thus be taken as a remarkable late medieval statement of Scotland's role as a distinct, but integral part of Catholic Europe. The clerestorey walls would originally have been plastered and painted with coloured decoration (cf Pluscarden, no. 46), thus linking the ceiling to the rest of the building.

Sacrament House, Deskford (no. 49)

Although the great pre-Reformation pulpit is now in King's College (see chapter 1), some other important furnishings remain, such as several fine tombs and a good series of modern stained glass windows, notably the Crombie and Bishops windows in the south aisle (by Douglas Strachan, 1908, 1913) and the fine, blue east window (by W Wilson, 1953).

The kirkyard is crammed with interesting tombs, from those of Bishop Dunbar (1533–the inspiration for the Tolquhon tomb, no. 43) and Bishop Lichton to that of Major Macpherson who was the Crown's agent for the suppression of human sacrifices in Orissa. 'Trades, Gentlemen, Church and University' are all represented, as well as the Aberdeen artist James Giles (1801-70).

49 Deskford Sacrament House, Kirkton of Deskford, Moray
AD 1551.
NJ 508616. In the Kirkton of Deskford, on side road E of B 9018 Keith/Cullen road.
HBM (SDD).

The rather plain, old kirk of Deskford stands near the heart of the lands of the powerful Ogilvie family, who rose to become Lords Deskford and finally Earls of Findlater and Seafield. Within the kirk is a finely carved late Gothic sacrament house presented by Alexander Ogilvie of that ilk and his wife in 1551. This small aumbry or recess was used for the reservation of the consecrated elements of the mass and is decorated with two angels holding a monstrance (in which the host was displayed), a running vine and side pinnacles. Of more modern, Renaissance, form are the scrolls for the inscription, the heraldry and the corbels. Presented by a local magnate, this is an example of the emphasis on personal salvation through church endowment that was a prominent feature of the late medieval church. Alexander Ogilvie and his wife are buried in Cullen collegiate church (no. 50), to which they also presented a sacrament house.

50* St Mary's Collegiate Church, Cullen, Moray

Mid 16th century AD.
NJ 507663. 1 km SW of the square in Cullen. Turn off Seafield Street at S end of Cullen into Seafield Place, second left into Cathay Terrace and first right down Old Church Road.

St Mary's, Cullen, is characteristic of the last phase of the medieval church in Scotland, which saw the foundation of many collegiate churches for the saying of masses for the souls of their benefactors. In 1536, a south aisle, endowed by Elena Hay, was added to a simple rectangular medieval church. In 1543 the chapel was raised to a collegiate church with endowment from, among others, Alexander Ogilvie of that ilk; the chancel was lengthened.

Ogilvie died in 1554 and his ornate tomb is in the chancel. It consists of a canopied recess containing an armour-clad effigy on top of a tomb-chest with weeping figures on its front. The crockets of the arch of the recess and the pinnacles above are all late Gothic in style. By contrast, the cherubs on the back wall of the recess and the medallion panels above are early Renaissance in inspiration. There is also a sacrament house (presented by Ogilvie) in the north wall.

The south wall of the chancel is occupied by a laird's loft of 1602, complete with armorial panels. It represents the continuing influence of the principal family (the Ogilvies, by then baronets) on the affairs and even the form of the kirk. On the north wall is a marble monument to one of the later Ogilvies, James, fourth earl of Findlater and Seafield, one of the architects of the Union of Parliaments in 1707.

The tombs, which were misappropriated and their dates recut by the second earl of Fife (see no. 2), have now been returned to Cullen.

Cullen old kirk (no. 50): the reformed layout of the interior dominated by the laird's loft

Castle Fraser (no. 21), from SW

The Tower of Drum (no. 31): the High Hall

Craigievar Castle (no. 20): 'six storeys of soft pink harl'

*Pluscarden Abbey (no. 46): the
north transept*

*St Machar's Cathedral, Aberdeen
(no. 48): the great ceiling, royal arms
of Scotland top left*

St Peter's Duffus and medieval market cross (no. 51)

Gilbert de Greenlaw's burial slab (1411) at Kinkell Church (no. 52)

52 Kinkell Church, Keithhall and Kinkell, Gordon

Early 16th century AD.
NJ 785190. 2 km S of Inverurie, off side road between Inverurie and Fintray.
HBM (SDD).

On the haughs of the Don are the broken remains of a characteristic early 16th century church, long and narrow, that was dedicated to St Michael. There is an unusual sacrament house, dated 1524, which was

51 St Peter's Church, Duffus, Moray

Late medieval and 18th century AD.
NJ 175686. 9 km NW of Elgin; turn E off B 9012 at Duffus PO.
HBM (SDD), market cross only.

The roofless remains of this typical 18th century church incorporate portions of much older work, including a fine early 16th century porch with groined vault and the base of the former tower (now the Sutherland burial vault). The stairs on the north side and the east end gave access to timber lofts.

St Peter's Cross, a typical medieval market cross, stands to the south, an indication of the days when markets were held regularly in such kirkyards. Some excellent table-tombs also survive, green and mossy.

113

probably designed by Canon Alexander Galloway, who may have been responsible for the ceiling of St Machar's (no. 48). This combines both Gothic and Renaissance elements (the latter in the inscription scrolls) in a way seen in various other north-east monuments throughout the 16th century. Beside it is a metal panel showing the crucifixion, also with Galloway's initials and the date 1525.

Within the church is the graveslab of Gilbert de Greenlaw, killed in the battle of Harlaw in 1411, which bears an unusually detailed carving of an armoured knight. This slab was reused by a Forbes in 1592.

53 St Ternan's Church, Arbuthnott, Kincardine and Deeside
13th, late 15th and 19th centuries AD.
NO 801746. 3 km NW of Inverbervie, on side road off B 967 Inverbervie/Auchenblae road.

This red sandstone medieval kirk rests on a quiet shelf above the Bervie Water. The oldest part is the chancel, which was dedicated by David de Bernham on 3 August 1242. The Lady Chapel, now the Arbuthnott Aisle, projects southwards from the chancel; this and the bell tower at the west end of the nave were built by Sir Robert Arbuthnott of that ilk in 1500. They are

St Ternan's, Arbuthnott (no. 53): Arbuthnott Aisle

St Ternan's, Arbuthnott (no. 53): the 13th century chancel

excellent examples of late medieval Scottish church architecture, with strong, tall buttresses and well-cut ashlar walls. Above the Lady Chapel is the Priest's Room, remarkably unspoiled, with stone window seats and a squint to the chapel.

The church was restored in 1896 by A Marshall Mackenzie, when the stained glass windows by Cottier were fitted into the chancel lancets. These,

representing Faith, Hope and Charity, are the 'three bit creatures of queans' mocked by the locals in *Sunset Song*, whose author, Lewis Grassic Gibbon, now lies in a corner of the kirkyard.

---

54 St Mary's Church, Auchindoir, Gordon
Late 13th century AD.
NJ 477245. 16 km NW of Alford, on B 9002.
HBM (SDD).

This simple rectangular church, set on a peaceful green mound, was built in the later 13th century as the parish church of Auchindoir, at a time when great efforts were being made to consolidate the parochial system. The south doorway is a fine example of work from this period, the high point of Scottish medieval stone-mason work. Its hood moulding is decorated with dogtooth carvings that surround the plain round-headed mouldings of the opening. The latter are carried on 'handsome crocket caps' and narrow shafts.

The church was remodelled in the early 16th century and a fine sacrament house, carved to look like a monstrance, inserted into a lancet window.

---

55 St Mary's Church, Monymusk, Gordon
Late 12th/early 13th century AD.
NJ 684152. In centre of Monymusk village, 10 km SW of Inverurie.

There has long been a Christian foundation at Monymusk. The community of Augustinian canons that Gilchrist, earl of Mar, established here in 1170 had, several centuries earlier, been preceded by a group of *Céli Dé*, servants of God, who were ultimately of Irish inspiration.

The present church incorporates two principal features of the Augustinian priory church; the simple west tower of thin coursed granite with sandstone

St Mary's, Auchindoir (no. 54): south door

St Mary's, Monymusk (no. 55): from SE (the original long chancel can be seen)

Mortlach Kirk (no. 56)

dressings, which now stands 15.5 m high (originally c 18 m), and the chancel arch with three shafts and cushion capitals. The original chancel was considerably longer than the present one, much of the remainder now being used as a burial enclosure. The crenellations on the tower are a poor 19th century addition.

Although much altered, the interior is light and pleasing; the Norman chancel arch provides a fine focus, and the wall monuments to successive Grant lairds repay study. There is some excellent modern stained glass (including an unusual depiction of the Monymusk Stone, *Céli Dé*, and Bennachie), and the Monymusk Stone itself, a Pictish symbol stone on which are carved a cross, a broken sword and a triple disc symbol.

56   Mortlach Parish Kirk, Dufftown, Moray
13th and 19th centuries AD.
NJ 323392. 0.7 km S of centre of Dufftown.

Mortlach is undoubtedly one of the earliest Christian sites in Grampian. Although it is not clear when the first shrine, chapel or hermitage was built, the (relatively late) tradition that at least three bishops had been based at Mortlach prior to 1140 is accepted by most scholars.

The present church, which is still set in a small kirkton distinct from the much later planned town, dates from the 13th century. The chancel, with its narrow lancets, survives from what would have been a simple rectangular medieval church. The present modified 'T' plan stems from the extensions of 1826 and 1876. It was restored in 1931.

As well as the quiet focus provided by the dark chancel, Mortlach's interior contains many interesting furnishings. In the north wall is an arched recess with effigy, the tomb of Alexander Leslie of Kininvie (d c 1549), while, opposite, is an unusual, if guileless, late 17th century monument to the Duffs of

Mortlach Kirk (no. 56): watch-house

Keithmore. The stained glass includes work by Cottier (chancel) and Strachan (south wall), the latter with recognisable local views and a Canadian theme. In the vestibule is an important early Pictish stone with beast and rare curvilinear symbol which may have been based on a brooch, as well as several fine tombstones.

The kirkyard is full of interest, including a little watch-house, a line of confident distillers' tombs and a Pictish stone, the Battle Stone, bearing on one side a cross between two fish monsters and a serpent, a bull's head and a horse and rider on the other.

57 Birnie Kirk, Elgin, Moray
Early 12th century AD.
NJ 206587. 4 km S of Elgin, on side road between New Elgin and B 9010 Elgin/Rafford road.

Dedicated to St Brendan and sitting on a prominent kirkyard mound, Birnie is one of the oldest places of worship in Moray. For a time before 1224, Birnie was one of the seats of the Bishops of Moray. Rectangular in plan, it has a short chancel, lit only by single lancets to north and south, but with no window to the east. The chancel is separated from the nave by a serene Romanesque arch with well preserved cushion capitals. The simple, rough font and the doorways to north and south are original; the nave was shortened (from the west) and the south windows enlarged in 1734. The restoration of 1891 was by A Marshall Mackenzie. The chancel lancets contain interesting modern glass.

In the kirkyard, beside the gate to the manse, is an early Pictish stone, incised with a simple eagle and a 'notched rectangle' and Z-rod.

Birnie Kirk (no. 57): the Romanesque arch

117

5

TRIBAL DEFENCE AND DISPLAY

The monuments that survive from Grampian's prehistoric past are considered in the next two chapters. The first stretches back in time from c 1000 AD to c 1200 BC, the second from then to the neolithic, c 4000 BC.

Picts and Romans

The people who inhabited the Grampian Region (and much of Scotland north of the Forth) between the 4th and the 9th centuries and who were regarded as Pictish by their neighbours, the Britons and the Anglo-Saxons, shared a similar militaristic and aristocratic culture which, in the case of the Picts, had origins in the Celtic iron age of the area. Pictish society was hierarchical, with a warrior aristocracy possibly of two sub-classes, cavalry and footmen, and a peasantry, in part bonded, all ruled by potentates. Geographical divisions also existed; in Grampian the Mounth and the Spey appear to have been important boundaries, the former more so, although the great province of Moray (which then extended far beyond its modern boundaries) retained a measure of independence long after the union of the Picts and the Scots in the mid 9th century.

The most important Pictish stronghold in Grampian was the great promontory fort of Burghead (no. 72) in Moray, which, with its well, its timber-laced wall of continental Celtic inspiration, and its fine bull stones, may be seen as a centre of royal power. This is

The triple ranks of banks and ditches crowning the Hill of Barra (no. 76)

emphasised by the other important, if not unique, Pictish sites nearby, the vivid and monumental Sueno's Stone (no. 59) and the mysterious Sculptor's Cave at Covesea (NJ 175707). Sueno's Stone may record a great victory over the Norse of Orkney; Burghead itself may have been attacked in the 9th century, while the other promontory forts along the Moray coast (notably Green Castle, Portknockie, NJ 488687; Castle Point, Troup, no. 73; and Dundarg, NJ 895649) were also occupied at this time.

Several of the landward hillforts of Grampian must also have been Pictish strongholds, although there has not been enough excavation to confirm this. The best candidate is the fort on the Mither Tap o' Bennachie (no. 74), in the heart of the Garioch, which has a stone wall with parapet clustered round a granite tor.

It is, however, by the fine series of symbol stones and cross-slabs that the Picts are most vividly represented in Grampian. Bearing a range of animal and object symbols that were current in everyday life in late Roman times (3rd-and 4th centuries AD), eg mirrors and combs, bronze cauldrons, swords, helmets, ladles, they may have begun to be erected as early as the 5th century. A broad sequence exists, but is complicated in Aberdeenshire by the late survival of certain forms. It begins with symbols incised on untreated boulders such as the Picardy Stone (no. 67), or the stones at Inveravon (no. 64), Broomend (no. 85), Newton House (NJ 662297), Inverurie (NJ 780206) or Tyrie

Pictish beast, Fyvie Kirk

Pictish symbol stone from Easterton of Roseisle, Moray

(NJ 930631). A decline in the quality of execution of some of the symbols suggests that they continued in use for some considerable time; compare the elegant crescent and V-rod at Broomend (no. 85) with the cruder example at Kintore (no. 66), or the fine, leaping muscular beast at Broomend with its lifeless counterpart at Fyvie (NJ 768377).

By the early 8th century a new series of stones appears; more elaborately dressed slabs bearing, in relief, a Christian cross as well as symbols that have been considerably reduced in importance in the composition. The earliest cross-slab in Grampian is probably that from Fordoun, now in the church at Auchenblae (NO 726784). Most of the north-east's cross-slabs, such as Dyce (no. 61), the Maiden Stone (no. 62), Brodie (no. 19), Migvie (no. 60) and, possibly,

Monymusk (no. 55) are regarded as late, perhaps as late as the second half of the 9th century. Such a dating would place them later than many cross-slabs with no Pictish symbols, such as Kinord (no. 58), which conventionally post-date symbol-bearing slabs, and into the period after the union of the Picts and Scots.

A great deal of debate has focused on the function that symbol stones performed in Pictish society. It is clear that at least some of them were involved in burial rituals, for example the Picardy Stone (no. 67) or the fine goose stone from Roseisle, Moray, now in the Royal Museum of Scotland. In such rituals the stones may have commemorated an ancestor, through his insignia of rank, the symbols, as well as providing his descendants with a form of title to the land—which invariably was of good agricultural quality. The proximity of symbol stones to sites of much earlier ritual importance is not fully understood (eg Ardlair stone circle, NJ 552279; Brandsbutt stone circle, no. 63; Broomend henge, no. 85; Covesea cave, NJ 175707; Rhynie barrow, NJ 497265). The occurrence of Pictish stones in many ancient kirkyards might result from the Christianisation of existing Pictish burial sites.

A few of the Pictish stones have inscriptions in ogam, an alphabet of combinations of short strokes invented in Ireland in the 4th century AD. The Grampian stones with early ogams (ie using the angle of a stone as the base line: Newton House, NJ 662297 and Auquhollie, NO 823908) are not accompanied by symbols, but the later examples are (Brandsbutt, no. 63; Logie Elphinstone, NJ 703258; Brodie, no. 19 and Formaston, Aboyne, now in Inverurie Museum).

The Picts appear in the writings of the Romans who encountered them in the first few centuries of our era. Of the Romans themselves, in Grampian they are represented by upstanding remains only at the marching camps of Raedykes (no. 68), Ythan Wells (NJ 655382) and, very sketchily, Kair House (NO 769768). The discovery of a large (57 ha) marching camp at Durno (NJ 698271) opposite Bennachie has led to the suggestion that the battle of Mons Graupius was fought here in AD 84. However, the case must remain, for the moment, unproven.

58 Kinord Cross-slab, Dinnet, Kincardine and Deeside

9th century AD.
NO 440997. 8 km W of Aboyne, in Muir of Dinnet National Nature Reserve (off B 9119) on N side of Loch Kinord.

This excellently preserved cross-slab of granite stands close to its original site. The interlace-filled cross occupies almost the whole surface of the slab, the arms in particular run up hard against the edges of the stone. The top panel bears four spiral knots and the angles of the cross have been hollowed out to emphasise the ring that embraces the angles. It is thus close to the free-standing ring-crosses of Irish inspiration seen in the west of Scotland.

Kinord Cross (no. 58)

59 Sueno's Stone, Cross-slab, Forres, Moray

9th century AD.
NJ 046595. At E end of Forres, on B 9011 Forres/Kinloss road.
HBM (SDD).

This, the tallest and most complex piece of early medieval sculpture in Scotland, most probably commemorates a heroic battle campaign, possibly against the Norse settlers of Orkney, by the men of Moray. The extensive province of Moray, from the 8th to the 12th century, retained considerable independence within the new kingdom. The stone has no connection with Swein Forkbeard who harried London in 994 and became king of Denmark (d 1014); it was given its misconceived name in 1726, probably shortly after it had been discovered, lying buried.

Standing over 6.5 m high, this 7.6 ton slab of sandstone was probably brought from the coast near Covesea, 15 km to the north-east. In many ways it is the culmination of several centuries of Pictish stone carving, while the organised narrative of its eastern face looks also to later complex tapestry stories, such as Bayeux.

The western face bears a relief carving of a great ring-headed cross whose shaft, rising from a horizontal base, is filled with interlace spiral knotwork. Below, two long, bearded figures confront each other, with smaller attendants behind. The sides are highly decorated, most notably on the upper half of the south side, where a vine scroll is inhabited, unusually, by little male figures which recall the imp-like figures in the *Book of Kells*.

The east face is divided into four panels of unequal length which can be read as a heroic narrative from top to bottom. The top panel (a line of figures above three lines of horsemen) shows a leader and his guard arriving on horseback for a battle. The top third of the great central panel shows the early medieval practice of fighting on foot; the upper line showing the leader flanked by his guard; the second row the single combat of the respective champions of both sides: note that the two left-most figures have turned to run away, denoting defeat. The third row shows a beseiged stronghold (probably a broch) and, on the left, the treatment meted out to the captured defenders: six headless corpses, their hands tied, and a pile of severed heads in front of the tower. Below the pile is a seventh body which has just been decapitated, the executioner holds the head in his left hand. The bottom row of this large panel shows the rout of the defeated force, the six

horses on the left fleeing from the infantry on the right. The third panel, with a curved object, perhaps a canopy, beneath which are piled more headless corpses and severed heads (including one in a little frame which may be the captured chief's) represents the final defeat of the enemy. The last panel, partially obscured by the modern base, shows the dispersal of the vanquished army.

This is war reporting on a monumentally self-confident scale.

Sueno's Stone (no. 59)

Migvie Stone (no. 60)

---

60 Migvie Stone, Cross-slab, Logie Coldstone, Kincardine and Deeside
9th century AD.
NJ 436068. 10 km N of Ballater, off A 97. In W side of kirkyard.

A roughly pointed pillar of gneiss, 2.1 m tall, bearing on one face a cross and on the back a horse and rider. As at nearby Kinord (no. 58), the cross fills the stone; it has, however, been carved with much less skill. In particular, the arms of the cross have been crammed in and the knot work in the top panel is distinctly jumbled. The cross is a waisted form, defined by a crude channel and filled with low-relief plait work. There are curious circular projections at the top and angles of the cross which perhaps suggest the suspension loops of a metal cross; two curves extend from the base in the manner of the scrolls at Kinord.

In the angles of the cross are three symbols and a horse and rider. The former are extremely small and rather crude; they comprise a horseshoe (rather than a crescent) and V-rod, a double disc and Z-rod and a pair of shears. The first and last symbols are unique to Aberdeenshire and may be very late. This, and the generally inferior quality of the carvings have led some scholars to suggest that this stone may have been sculpted later even than the Kinord cross (no. 58). It is, nonetheless, an oddly moving monument.

61 Chapel of St Fergus, Symbol Stone and Cross-slab, Dyce, Aberdeen

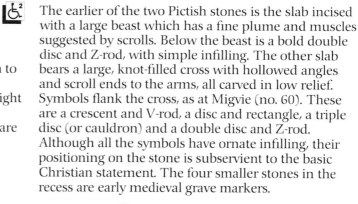

7th and 9th centuries AD.
NJ 875154. 2 km NW of Dyce. On A 947 immediately S of bridge over Don, turn W on to minor road, cross old railway line, turn right (Kinaldie), pass under present railway, keep right and in 0.6 km turn right (N) over railway (signposted). Follow track for 0.6 km. Stones are in east gable of old kirk.
HBM (SDD).

The earlier of the two Pictish stones is the slab incised with a large beast which has a fine plume and muscles suggested by scrolls. Below the beast is a bold double disc and Z-rod, with simple infilling. The other slab bears a large, knot-filled cross with hollowed angles and scroll ends to the arms, all carved in low relief. Symbols flank the cross, as at Migvie (no. 60). These are a crescent and V-rod, a disc and rectangle, a triple disc (or cauldron) and a double disc and Z-rod. Although all the symbols have ornate infilling, their positioning on the stone is subservient to the basic Christian statement. The four smaller stones in the recess are early medieval grave markers.

Incised symbols, Dyce (no. 61)

Relief symbols, Dyce (no. 61)

124

The Maiden Stone (no. 62): west face

62 Maiden Stone, Cross-slab, Chapel of Garioch, Gordon

9th century AD.
NJ 703247. 7 km W of Inverurie, on side road passing through hamlet of Chapel of Garioch to S of A 96.
HBM (SDD).

Named from the legend of the daughter of the laird of Balquhain who died during her elopement, this is a cool, pink slab of granite, bearing on one face, in low relief, a most elaborate and confident ring-headed cross and on the other four bold symbols, carved in high relief. Above the cross on the west face two fish monsters surround a man with arms outstretched (a Calvary scene?). Below the cross a great roundel with spiral work surrounded by interlace, key-pattern and knotwork can still be discerned. The sides of the slab have also been carefully decorated. The east face has been divided into four panels, bearing a centaur (?), a notched rectangle (?based on a gate tower) and Z-rod, a Pictish beast and a mirror and double-sided comb. These have all been carved with a 'massive simplicity' that was an elegant and successful response to the problem of executing relief sculpture in granite.

The cross, the treatment of the symbols and their framing in separate panels on the back of the stone all suggest that this was one of the last symbol stones to be carved in Grampian. It is certainly one of the finest.

63 Brandsbutt, Symbol Stone, Inverurie, Gordon

6th/7th century AD.
NJ 759224. In N end of Inverurie, off Burghmuir Drive (which links Blackhall Road and A 96): turn up Brankie Road, the stone is at the corner of Gordon Terrace.
HBM (SDD).

A great, grey slab, once broken up but now restored, bearing an incised crescent and V-rod, a fine, scaley serpent and Z-rod with simple terminals, all carved in a broad confident line. Running up the left hand side of the stone is a typical Pictish ogam inscription in which the guide-line has been drawn in. It can be transliterated IRATADDOARENS, which may be similar to the Newton House stone (NJ 662297) IDDARRNNN. This has been linked with Eddarrnonn, a possible rendering of St Ethernanus. It reinforces the interpretation of the symbol stones as some form of personal memorial.

The stone is adjacent to the site of a stone circle, now marked out in the grass.

The Brandsbutt Stone (no. 63)

125

St Peter's, Inveravon (no. 64)

Pictish beast's head, Rhynie (no. 65)

64 St Peter's Church, Symbol Stones, Inveravon, Moray

6th/7th century AD.
NJ 182375. 10 km SW of Aberlour, off A 95.
Stones are mounted on outside S wall of church.

A group of four incised symbol stones found in the kirkyard. They are typical early Pictish stones, being incised on rough, unprepared boulders. Starting at the west, the first bears a crescent (with simple infilling) and V-rod, a triple disc and bar (the 'cauldron symbol') and a mirror and comb. Number 2 is a small fragment of a most graceful beast's head, while no. 3 bears a great disc and rectangle above a fine eagle and a rather rudimentary mirror and comb, all deeply and confidently cut. The last stone has a rather worn crescent and V-rod over a plain beast.

65 Rhynie Old Kirkyard, Symbol Stones, Rhynie, Gordon

6th/7th century AD.
NJ 499265. 13 km S of Huntly, at entrance to kirkyard (approached down narrow track E of A 97, at S end of Rhynie).

Two early Pictish stones, the larger, of gabbro, incised with a fine beast's head (resembling an otter or seal), a double disc and Z-rod and a mirror and comb. The comb is of a particular type which may be as early as the 4th or 5th century, while the surviving terminal of the Z-rod is more usually found on certain V-rods.

The small slab of pink granite has part of an incised double disc and Z-rod, a crescent and V-rod and a mirror, all in a very simple style.

A total of eight Pictish stones comes from the immediate vicinity of the kirkyard, perhaps focused on the Craw Stane, a substantial slab incised with a fish and a beast, which still stands on the hill shoulder above (NJ 497263).

66 Kintore Church, Symbol Stone, Kintore, Gordon

6th/7th century AD.
NJ 793162. Inside gate of kirkyard in centre of Kintore, at junction of A 96 and B 977.

This incised Pictish stone, 1.2 m tall, is unusual in having symbols on both faces. Differences in technique may indicate that they were carved at different times. A rather crude crescent and V-rod are placed above an almost lifeless beast on one face, whereas on the other a confidently carved fish surmounts a fine triple disc and cross bar. The interpretation of this last symbol as representing a bronze ring-handled cauldron suspended on a cross bar can be seen from the way the bar crosses over the inner edges of the rings and beneath their outer edges.

Kintore (no. 66): fish and cauldron symbols

Kintore (no. 66): crescent and beast symbols

67 Picardy Stone, Symbol Stone, Insch, Gordon

♿L3

6th/7th century AD.
NJ 609302. 3 km NW of Insch off minor road to Largie; signposted off B 992 in Insch.
HBM (SDD).

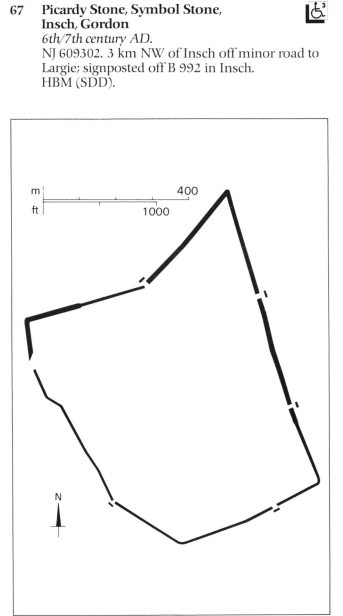

Raedykes (no. 68)

This rough whinstone pillar, standing 1.98 m high, bears three finely incised symbols and is unusual in being, apparently, still in its original location. The symbols are on the south face and consist of a well drawn double disc and Z-rod, the latter with ornate, flame-like, terminal over a tightly coiled serpent and Z-rod with a simple mirror beneath. (There is no comb.) The essentially prehistoric, remote quality of the Pictish symbols can be gauged here.

An 'excavation' in 1856 found that the stone stood on a low cairn, 1.9 m in diameter, which had an extended grave beneath its perimeter; this emphasises the association between symbol stones and burial and property rights.

68 Raedykes Roman Camp, Stonehaven, Kincardine and Deeside

♿L3

1st century AD.
NO 841902. 5.5 km NW of Stonehaven, N off A 957, on first minor road to Riding School; turn right again on to another back road and in 1 km park at track to Broomhill Cottage. Camp lies to N.

This, the best preserved Roman earthwork in Grampian, is irregular in plan in order to make best use of the terrain. Much of the circuit of rampart and ditch, which encloses 37 ha, can still be seen in good condition on the eastern, seaward slopes of Garrison Hill. The temporary, or 'marching' camp was probably built in AD 83 or 84 during the brief campaign conducted by Gnaeus Julius Agricola, governor of the Roman province of Britain, against the Caledonians, which culminated in the battle of Mons Graupius.

A large earth and stone bank, 180 m long and up to 4.5 m thick and 1.2 m high, with a ditch, lies in woodland 230 m S of the camp (at NO 843896) and parallel to the rampart. It may have acted as a defensive outwork.

Mortlach Kirk (no. 56): stained glass representations of Céli Dé and the two Pictish stones found in the kirkyard

Maiden Stone (no. 62): east face

Picardy Stone (no. 67)

Eslie the Greater recumbent stone circle (no. 92)

FORTS AND FIELDS

The defended settlements of Grampian, built as they were over nearly two millennia, are found in a confusing variety of forms and locations. Only one type, the promontory fort, has been excavated and dated to modern standards.

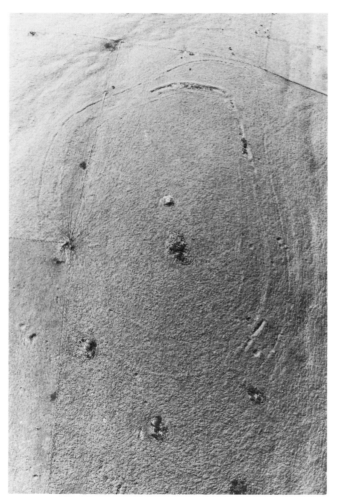

Unfinished fort, Durn Hill, Portsoy

Simple stockades, such as Hill of Christ's Kirk (NJ 601274) or small enclosures defined either by a single rampart and ditch (eg Wheedlemont, no. 77, Middle Knox, Gourdon, NO 817702) or a rough stone wall (eg Cairnmore, NJ 503249, Mortlich, NJ 535017, North Keig, NJ 599200) are the basic types. They were often sited without much thought for covering dead ground (Wheedlemont; North Keig) or were very sketchily defended (eg the large enclosure at Tillymuick, NJ 649245).

However, stronger and much more ostentatious structures are also found, such as the triple banks and ditches which were succeeded by a pair of stone walls on the Barmekin of Echt (NJ 726071) or Hill of Barra (no. 76). The most assertive structures were those oblong forts with high stone walls laced with timber baulks, such as Tap o'Noth (no. 78), Dunnideer (no. 75) or Doune of Relugas (NJ 003495). A more modest example is at Cairnton of Balbegno (NO 633722). Now reduced to fused masses of glassy stone or grey cindery screes, their firing was a deliberate act by successful attackers.

Several forts in Grampian have been described as unfinished. While the defensive circuits round the (?)earlier oblong fort of Dunnideer (no. 75) may have been completed by stockades, not now visible, genuine marker trenches can be seen on Durn Hill, Portsoy (NJ 571638), Little Conval, Dufftown (NJ 294392) and Knockargetty Wood, Cromar (NJ 454030). Such trenches marked out the planned line of the defences, and they survive only where building was never completed.

Finally, there is an important series of coastal promontory forts, which show evidence of occupation during the first millennium BC and the first millennium AD. The great Pictish fortress of Burghead (no. 72) is exceptional, both in size (3 ha) and richness of material culture. More typical are Cullykhan (no.

73), Green Castle, Portknockie (NJ 488687) and Dundarg, Aberdour (NJ 895649).

A question prompted by many steep climbs to cold windy ramparts is how did these forts function as aristocratic centres, and in which seasons? Even before the climatic changes of the mid first millennium it is difficult to conceive of wintering on Tap o'Noth; it might be that lower altitude enclosures such as that found near the kirkyard at Rhynie were used.

The early farming settlements of the region are similarly poorly dated. The earlier type, beginning perhaps in the second millennium, is represented by scatters of stone clearance heaps and the occasional

hut circle (the circular footings of a house) as at Balnagowan (no. 79), Aitnoch (NH 985383), Tom na Glein (NJ 208369) or Bellmuir (NJ 870365). The settlements of Old and New Kinord (nos 71, 70) are different from these earlier, open types in being more compartmentalised. Large-scale stock control with some agriculture are represented by these remains. The souterrains, underground storehouses for agricultural and pastoral products, date from the end of the first millennium BC and indicate similar organisation of farming by this time.

---

69   Culsh Souterrain, Tarland, Kincardine and Deeside
Early 1st millennium AD.
NJ 504054. 7 km N of Aboyne, on B 9119 (torch at farm).
HBM (SDD).

This souterrain, or underground storehouse, shows the characteristic curved plan, 14.3 m long and 1.8 m wide and high at the inner end. It was constructed by digging a trench into the rocky subsoil, lining it with drystone walling and roofing it with substantial stone slabs. When it was cleared out c 1850 it was found to be filled 'nearly to the top with ... a rich unctuous earth' which suggests that it had been infilled deliberately, like souterrains further south. There is a cup-mark near the base of the north wall.

The visitor scrambles into the darkness, pressed by the lintels towards the floor. On rounding the curve, the passage opens up and out into a round-ended space. The stillness of the air and the evenness of the temperature inside Culsh suggest that such structures are best interpreted as storehouses; the adjoining timber house which it served presumably lay just upslope. A considerable quantity of agricultural produce could be stored in this structure, which perhaps indicates some centralisation of the control of food by later prehistoric times.

Culsh souterrain (no. 69): interior

130

70 New Kinord Settlement, Dinnet, Kincardine and Deeside

Late 1st millennium BC.

NJ 449001. 8 km W of Aboyne, in Muir of Dinnet National Nature Reserve, entered off B 9119, 1.4 km N of Dinnet. Settlement lies c 75 m up track opposite carpark.

New Kinord settlement (no. 70): Ogston's plan

New Kinord settlement (no. 70): aerial view in winter

A settlement of stone-walled houses, stock enclosures and droveways, this site was systematically recorded by Sir Alexander Ogston, sometime physician to Queen Victoria. The contiguous structures, A, B and E on Ogston's plan have been interpreted as houses. A is massively walled and sunken-floored, a sizeable 19 m in diameter. B appears to consist of a hut circle enclosed by a stone wall 18 m in diameter. E is 17 m in diameter and similar to B in plan, but is slighter in construction (and may represent the remains of a timber house). The souterrain, C, appears to open off E (?with a connection to B as well).

The enclosures, R and D, lie to the N and S of the three huts. D is contiguous with A and 19.5 m in diameter; it has a clearly defined entrance to the E. R is not attached to any house but one massive main wall of the surrounding field system runs north from its north-western corner. R is more irregular in plan, being 26 m E-W by 24 m N-S; its entrance faces south-west. The double walls, M, have been interpreted as a droveway. The other features, X, Y, etc are more vestigial.

The birch woods around contain many stone banks and walls of a sizeable system of large enclosures, related to this well organised, prestigious farmstead.

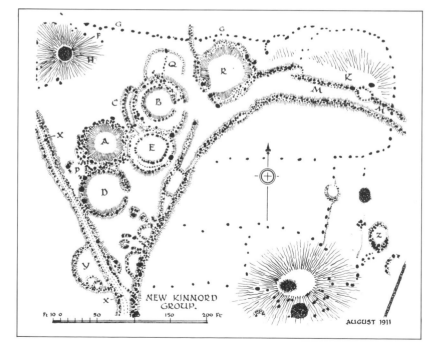

71   Old Kinord Settlement, Dinnet, Kincardine and Deeside

Late 1st millennium BC.

NJ 444002. 8.5 km W of Aboyne, in Muir of Dinnet National Nature Reserve, entered off B 9119, 1.4 km N of Dinnet. Cross track from carpark, walk through birches (past New Kinord settlement, no. 70), to clearing, turn left (W) and go through birches for c 250 m.

This is an enclosed settlement surrounded by a system of large fields represented by stone banks and clearance heaps. The most substantial features are A and B on Ogston's plan which have stone walls, 2.5 m thick, sunken floors and diameters of 16.5 m and 17.5 m. Their entrances face east and north respectively. A small souterrain, C, can be seen clearly, opening off feature D which may be a house site similar to feature E at New Kinord (no. 70). In 1904,

the Hon J Abercromby excavated huts H, B, A, and D and found a stone disc, flints, charcoal, pottery and a quern fragment. His conclusion that the structures were late cattle kraals was dismissed trenchantly, but probably rashly, by Ogston as 'untenable'.

Features L and K are enclosures, less substantial than D and R at New Kinord. Although structure H was interpreted as a hut it lies outside the main enclosure wall and is irregular in plan. A re-excavation of structure D produced no datable finds. However, a burnt hazelnut shell indicated woodland foraging, while soil pollen analysis suggested the existence of extensive pasture and some cereals.

Loch Kinord, over the ridge to the south, contains one of the few crannogs or lake dwellings in Grampian. It is the smallest islet in the loch, an oval, pile- and stone-built feature, 22 m by 19 m.

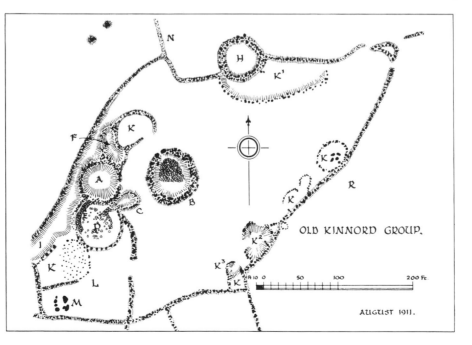

Old Kinord settlement (no. 71): Ogston's plan

Burghead Bull (no. 72)

Burghead fort (no. 72): plan

72 Burghead, Promontory Fort and Well, Burghead, Moray

1st millennium AD.
NJ 109691. 11 km NW of Elgin, at seaward end of modern village.
HBM (SDD) (well only).

The modern traveller, fighting for breath and warmth in a gale on the headland of Burghead, may find it difficult to believe that he is standing in one of the most magnificent centres of Pictish power. Such was the destruction caused by the building of the present village in 1805-9, that the visitor must recreate in his mind the three great lines of rampart, with timber reinforcing, that stood 6 m high and ran across the neck of the promontory from Young Street to Bath Street.

In 1809 the rampart that (most characteristically for a Dark Age site) formed the seaward defences was observed to consist of '... the most various materials, viz, masses of stone with lime, cement, pieces of pottery and baked bricks and tiles, half burnt beams of wood, broken cornices and mouldings of well-cut freestone.... On some pieces of the freestone are seen remains of mouldings and carved figures, particularly of a bull, very well executed.... [These were] the ruins ... of a considerable town'. The 'bull, very well executed' is a reference to the famous Pictish animal carvings from Burghead, of which six survive,* although between 25 and 30 are recorded in the literature.

A small stump of the innermost cross rampart survives in the 'Doorie Hill', the green mound on which sits the blackened mounting for the Clavie (the midwinter fire-festival). The upper and lower wards of the fort also survive, the rampart of the latter being the best preserved (it is from this wall that evidence for nailing of the timber beams in the wall comes). In all, nearly 3 ha were enclosed, making Burghead one of the largest forts of any date in Scotland. The possibility that the boats of the Pictish 'navy' that carried the men of Moray in battle to Orkney sheltered beneath the headland cannot be ignored.

The Well is an elaborate subterranean rock-cut basin, with walkway around; it was damaged on discovery. Although described in the past as a 'Roman' well or an early Christian baptistry, its location in an elaborate Pictish fort suggests that its unusual construction is merely a reflection of the overall level of grandeur required by the inhabitants for their water supply. Alternatively, it could have functioned as a water shrine, ultimately of Celtic inspiration.

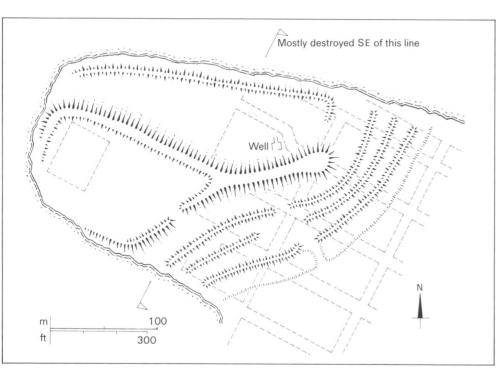

Mostly destroyed SE of this line

Well

N

m ⊢――――――――――― 100
ft ⊢――――――――――― 300

Two are in Burghead Library, two are in Elgin Museum and the Royal Museum of Scotland and the British Museum have one each.

73 Castle Point, Troup (Cullykhan), Promontory Fort, Pennan, Banff and Buchan

Early 1st millennium BC-18th century AD.
NJ 838661. 16 km W of Fraserburgh. Turn N off B 9031 on track W of steep den of Tore of Troup.

Excavation on this low coastal headland of conglomerate has revealed an extraordinarily long sequence of occupation. The defensive properties of the site are emphasised by the walk to it, along a narrow knife-edged isthmus, nowhere more than 4 m wide.

The initial defence was on the Knoll, the landward point of the promontory, and consisted of at least one palisade, probably built in the early 1st millennium BC. Around the 4th century BC, the Knoll was refortified with a vertical wall of stone and timber and an elaborate gateway, similar to some German forts. Considerable evidence of metalworking as well as objects such as an imported German chisel lay behind this defence. The next phase occurred sometime after 100 BC, further east (between the Knoll and the medieval castle), and consisted of a timber-laced rampart which was destroyed by a fierce fire. A fourth phase saw the cutting of two flat-bottomed ditches across the promontory at the junction of the Knoll and the main area.

From the objects recovered in the excavation and the defensive phases outlined above, it is possible to summarise the prehistoric occupations as a late bronze-age refuge, an iron-age citadel and an early Pictish fort. Subsequently the promontory was used for a medieval castle and for Fort Fiddes, an 18th century shore defence.

Castle Point, Troup (no. 73)

74 Mither Tap o' Bennachie, Hillfort, Inverurie, Gordon

1st millennium AD.
NJ 682223. 9 km W of Inverurie. Carpark signposted S off the minor road running S of the A 96 through Chapel of Garioch; a fairly arduous climb of c 2 km.

The most easterly of the granite tors of the evocative Bennachie massif rises to the not inconsiderable height of 518 m and is flanked by an unusual stone-walled fort. About 30 m below the summit the main wall, c 7 m wide and up to 1.7 m high, of drystone construction, can be seen. A triangular annexe lies to the west of the entrance which itself is in the north-eastern arc of the wall. The elaborate entrance runs for 16 m, extending into the fort. Traces of a parapet on the wallhead can be seen on either side of the entrance passage. (Visitors are requested not to climb on the walls.) An inner wall is represented by tumble and scree around the main tor. A well or cistern is against the south arc of the outer wall, while a second entrance may have been on the south-western circuit. Excavations in the 1870s revealed up to 10 hut foundations, several of which must have represented secondary occupation as they had been built on top of stones fallen from the ruined wall.

The area to the north of Bennachie has been claimed as the site of the battle of Mons Graupius in AD 84 on the basis of a large temporary Roman camp found at Durno (NJ 698271). However, the construction of the Mither Tap fort around the rocky outcrops of the summit has more in common with early historic practices than with iron-age traditions.

Mither Tap o' Bennachie (no. 74): aerial view

135

Dunnideer hillfort (no. 75): aerial view

Dunnideer, Hillfort, Insch, Gordon
1st millennium BC.
NJ 612281. 2 km W of Insch, on minor road
from Insch to Clashindarroch Forest.

At least two phases of prehistoric defences crown this
prominent hill which rises to 268 m OD on the west
of the Garioch. The medieval tower was built c 1260,
partly from prehistoric stonework and is one of the
earliest stone castles in Scotland. Three outer, sketchy,
lines of defence have been interpreted as an
unfinished fort, probably secondary to the hilltop
enclosure. The central line (D on plan), on the hill
flanks c 60 m down from the summit, is the clearest,
being represented by a rampart and ditch at the WSW
and ESE, linked by slight marker trenches. The inner
and outer lines (C and E) are only evident as breaks of
slope in certain areas.

The summit defences consist of two stone walls, the
outer (B) being a low stony bank, clearest on the east
and absent on the south. The inner (A) represents the
vitrified fort, an oblong enclosure 65 m by 25 m, with
no clear entrance. The intensity of the burning that
caused the vitrification can be seen in the fused masses
of stone lying to north and south; impressions of the
burnt-out timbers can be seen in places. A depression
under the south-eastern corner of the castle is
probably the cistern for the fort.

Seven hut platforms are scooped into the slopes
c 45 m downslope to north and south of the summit,
five on the south and two on the north. The largest is
12 m by 7.5 m. They probably pre-date the unfinished
fort as its marker line (D) respects the outer rim of one
of the southern platforms.

Opposite Dunnideer, on Hill of Christ's Kirk
(NJ 601274), are the remains of another unfinished
fort represented by three marker trenches enclosing a
palisade slot 40 m in diameter.

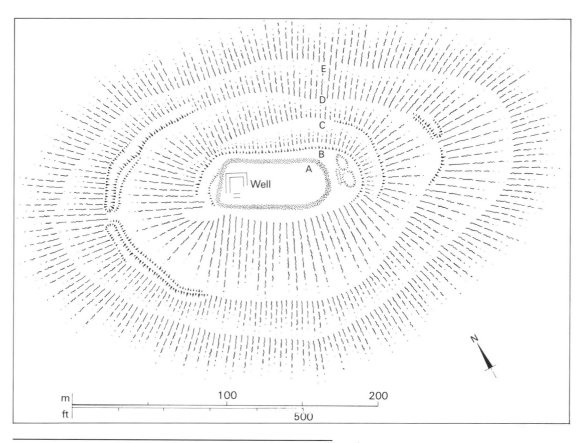

Dunnideer hillfort (no. 75): plan

76 Hill of Barra, Hillfort, Oldmeldrum, Gordon

1st millennium BC.

NJ 802257. 1.5 km S of Oldmeldrum. Walk up track opposite Barra Castle (on B 9170 Oldmeldrum/Inverurie road) for c 1.4 km.

The fort on this 193 m OD grassy hill appears to be of two phases represented by a pair of ramparts and ditches surrounding a (?later) stone-walled enclosure. The defences are best preserved in the north and north-east, where the ramparts are a maximum of 2 m high. The outer defences reduce to one line on the craggy west side; there is an additional, outer bank and ditch on the north-west. The single entrance is at the east, where a 4 m wide passage, edged with stones, runs through all three lines of defence. (The gap on the north is recent.)

The presence of a wood on the hill until the 19th century has ensured the survival of the medieval rig and furrow cultivation on the summit and northern slopes. There is a tradition that John Comyn, earl of Buchan, camped here before his defeat at the hands of Bruce in the battle of Barra in 1307.

137

77 Cnoc Cailliche (Wheedlemont), Hillfort, Rhynie, Gordon
1st millennium BC.
NJ 472260. 16 km S of Huntly on minor road from Rhynie to Craig.

This oval enclosure, which crowns a shoulder of the rounded, 352 m OD hill near the top of Strathbogie, is typical of the simple later prehistoric forts of Grampian. It consists of a shallow ditch, 4 m wide and 1 m deep, with a stony bank on its inner edge and a slight bank on the outer edge. The entrance is at the north-eastern end. The subdued defences and the dead ground surrounding the fort, especially to north and east, suggest that defence was not an overwhelming priority for the builders.

Cnoc Cailliche fort (no. 77)

78 Tap o'Noth, Hillfort, Rhynie, Gordon
1st millennium BC—early 1st millennium AD.
NJ 484293. 11 km S of Huntly: a strenuous walk of up to 2 km is involved, starting at the track end on the A 941 Rhynie/Dufftown road, 200 m W of Scurdargue.

Two defensive episodes have been identified on this most spectacular hillfort which is, at 563 m OD, the second highest in Scotland (after Ben Griam Beg in Sutherland, at 620 m). The larger, and possibly earlier, enclosure covers a massive 21 ha and consists of an outwork, a stony wall with a core of boulders, running round the break of slope on all but the steepest south-eastern side. At least 145 platforms have been found within this enclosure, as well as substantial tracks. The platforms are most numerous on the north-east and north-west sides. Although some of the larger ones are on the more southerly slopes, the concentration on the north side may be the result of the prevailing wind. It is presumed that many of the platforms (at least near the upper fort) must be quarries; nevertheless, the existence of any hut sites at this altitude and their relative remoteness from good agricultural land suggest a date no later than the early first millennium BC, before the climate deteriorated. The site is, however, formally undated, although three glass beads and other late iron-age finds came from very close to this lower enclosure.

The upper fort consists of a truly massive wall, vitrified extremely heavily in places, enclosing a rectangular area 105 m by 40 m. When the wall was excavated in 1891, it was found to be from 6 m to 8 m wide at the base and to rise to 3.5 m in height. The cistern, at the south end of the fort, was found to be 2.2 m deep. The severe vitrification could only have been produced by substantial quantities of timber and brushwood; once alight the fort must have been visible as a glowing beacon for days. It is not known when, or by whom, this great work, at once of defence and of display, was destroyed.

Tap o'Noth (no. 78): the great wall

79 Balnagowan Field System, Tarland, Kincardine and Deeside

Early 1st millennium BC.

NJ 494007. 3 km NW of Aboyne, on B 9094 Aboyne/Tarland road, turn W onto track just S of Mill of Gellan. Walk up track for 1 km to Muir Cottage, turn right (W) and enter rough pasture (gates/stock); field system lies on east face of Craig Dhu and runs over much of Balnagowan Hill (in woodland).

This is one of the most extensive systems of stone clearance heaps in Grampian, extending over 145 ha on the hill shoulder and flanks of Balnagowan Hill. Although much is now masked by afforestation, it is still possible to appreciate the extent of the land clearance carried out by the farmers of the first millennium BC. The clearance heaps are larger than usual in the north-east, from 6 to 12 m in diameter, while the field banks can also be traced.

The earlier long cairn (no. 104) sits on the saddle amidst the system.

*Circle of the moon: Strichen
recumbent stone circle (no. 93)*

6

ANCESTORS OF ANCESTORS

The earliest monuments left to us in Grampian, the henges, cairns and stone circles of the first farmers and their descendants, are ceremonial or funerary in nature (although it is unlikely that prehistoric man made such a firm distinction between the ritual or religious and the practical or domestic as we do today). By contrast, little is known of their settlements, barring the great timber hall at Balbridie on Deeside (NO 733959). Built by sophisticated carpenters, it was 24.5 m long by 13 m wide (320 square m internally) and rose 8.5 m to a roof ridge. It appears to have been a substantial house-cum-barn for an extended family of farmers.

The sites described here display several features that can be traced over a considerable period. Some are minor, such as the recurrent use of quartzite at Clava cairns, recumbent stone circles and the later kerb cairns. Others, like the emphasis on the south-west in the alignment of such monuments, are more fundamental. The significance of these, and other, elements, is explored below.

CAIRNS AND CISTS

Round cairns and short stone cists were mostly built during the early part of the bronze age, the second millennium BC; they are the burial places of individuals of considerable importance in their communities. One of the means by which status could be acquired during this period was through the

control of the production and distribution of prestige goods, whether metal objects (eg daggers, earrings), or fine beaker pottery. Such high-status burials were often placed in elaborately constructed short cists, stone-lined graves, c 1 m in length, into which the

Symbol of power: beaker pot from Skene

141

Logie Newton (no. 80): quartzite kerb cairn

body of the grandee or member of his family was placed, the knees drawn up to the chin, and accompanied by a beaker and sometimes also by objects of flint, fine stone or jet and amber. There are good reconstructions of such short cist beaker burials in the Anthropological Museum, Marischal College, Aberdeen, in James Dun's House, Schoolhill, Aberdeen and in the Tolbooth Museum, Stonehaven.

Many cists would have been covered only by a small mound of upcast soil, but others were sealed by more substantial above-ground structures. Great round cairns of grey, bare stones were built in conspicuous,

skyline, locations (eg Tullos Hill, no. 83; Cairn Crescent, West Cults, NJ 883028; the Slacks, Kirkhill, NJ 841144; Cairn Fichlie, NJ 458148; the Law of Melrose, NJ 756642), or turf and earth barrows, some sizeable like Forglen (NJ 698509). Some round cairns were very simple, eg Philla Cairn (NO 789710); others were rather more complex, eg Canterland (NO 706653) or White Cow Wood (NJ 947519).

A general trend in such structures during the second millennium was a reduction in overall size; this is seen most clearly in the kerb cairns which come towards the end of the sequence of monuments.

80 Logie Newton, Kerb Cairns, Auchterless, Banff and Buchan

Late 2nd millennium BC.
NJ 659391. 13 km E of Huntly; on side road between B 9001 and Wells of Ythan. Walk up hill for c 1 km, along field boundaries from Logie Newton farm.

The three small, unearthly, rings of quartzite blocks that glisten in the sleet and sparkle in the sun high on the south facing shoulder of Kirk Hill represent two trends in the burial and ritual monuments of Grampian that run back over 1500 years. The first, seen here in the diameters of the rings of between 6 and 7 m, is the gradual reduction in the size of the feature (compare the great single ring cairn at Loanhead, no. 98). The second is the use of quartzite, a notable characteristic of the earlier recumbent stone circles and Clava cairns, at Logie Newton translated into hefty blocks up to 1.3 m in length. Kerb cairns are often found in groups, as here, and their kerbstones are frequently disproportionately large when compared with the flat interiors of the cairns. There are few, however, so striking or so dramatically unreal as this Buchan group.

The location of the Roman marching camp of Ythan Wells on the hill to the south (NJ 655382) can be appreciated from the kerb cairns.

81 Memsie, Round Cairn, Rathen, Banff and Buchan

Early 2nd millennium BC.
NJ 976620. 5 km S of Fraserburgh. Signposted S off B 9032 0.7 km E of its junction with the A 981 Fraserburgh/Strichen road.
HBM (SDD).

This great cairn of bare stones, 24 m in diameter and 4.4 m high, is the sole survivor of a cemetery of three mighty cairns that once clustered on the long low ridge of Cairn Muir. Its plain, unadorned, profile and absence of vegetation are typical of the larger bronze-age cairns of Grampian.

82 Bucharn, Round Cairn, Strachan, Kincardine and Deeside

Early 2nd millennium BC.
NO 659929. 5 km SW of Banchory. Turn N off B 976 1.5 km W of Strachan on to back road; in 0.6 km walk up farm track through Bucharn steading and along field edges (0.6 km) to cairn.

This massive round cairn of bare stones is spectacularly sited at the edge of a hill terrace with wide views across the River Feugh and up into the Forest of Birse. It is 27 m in diameter and 4.5 m high, but the platform on which it sits is probably the result of field clearance and ploughing. The cairn is intervisible with another of similar size c 1 km to the east (NO 668933), while the dyke immediately to the east runs over a smaller cairn.

Bucharn round cairn (no. 82)

83 Tullos Hill, Round Cairns, Loirston, Aberdeen

Early 2nd millennium BC.
NJ 957036. 3 km SE of centre of Aberdeen. Cross Victoria Bridge to Torry, turn left into South Esplanade East, then Sinclair Road; at Nigg Bay turn right (S) and after crossing railway park in Model Farm carpark; ascend hill to Crab's Cairn.

The ridge which forms the skyline of the seaward-facing Tullos and Doonies Hills bears the remains of an important cairn cemetery of the bronze age. Four round cairns survive in varying conditions (the adjacent rubbish tip is gradually being landscaped).

Crab's Cairn (NJ 963037) is well positioned with wide views to the sea; it has, however, sustained some damage and is incorporated into a field boundary. It is 14 m in diameter and 1.7 m high. 500 m to the west, along the field boundary, lies Baron's Cairn (NJ 957036) in a prominent skyline position on a knoll. It is 18 m in diameter and 1.7 m high and bears a trig point. 800 m to the south-west, along the ridge, is Cat Cairn (NJ 951031); now somewhat altered, it was originally 22 m by 19 m and 2.5 m high. A possible platform survives on the north and south.

These three cairns are intervisible; the fourth, Tullos Cairn (NJ 959040), is not. It lies 425 m down slope to the north-east from Baron's Cairn (head for the group of three tower blocks) on a whin- and heather-covered shelf with a view seaward to the north. This cairn of bare stones, 20 m in diameter and 2.5 m high, is still a considerable landscape feature.

84 Cairn o'Mount, Round Cairn, Fettercairn, Kincardine and Deeside

Early 2nd millennium BC.
NO 649806. 15 km S of Banchory, on B 974 Banchory/Fettercairn road, immediately S of summit of the pass.

This fine hilltop cairn is 15.5 m in diameter and 3.5 m high. It is typical of several skyline cairns which have been added to and altered by generations of travellers.

Cairn o'Mount (no. 84)

CIRCLES OF THE MOON

Within the neolithic heartland of the north-east of Scotland there developed during the third millennium BC a unique type of megalithic monument, the recumbent stone circle, whose precise dating and relationship to other ritual monuments within Britain and Ireland are still debated. The recumbent stone circle can be described briefly as a circle of standing stones, from 18.2 m to 24.4 m in diameter, whose two tallest members are on the south-western arc, flanking a massive slab, with an average weight of 24 tons, which has been laid on its side and carefully chocked up to level its upper surface. Of the 99 certain or probable recumbent stone circles in Grampian, 74 can be accepted as definite sites; many were damaged by agricultural improvements. The circles described here have been chosen for their completeness and their accessibility and to demonstrate the variety of plans that developed during the millennium or more during which they were in vogue.

Recumbent stone circles are usually found on the crests of hills or terraces, with wide southerly views. At some, the first work of construction involved the levelling or terracing of the site (eg Loanhead, no. 98; Castle Fraser, NJ 714125; Berrybrae, NK 027571). It is likely that the first stones to be erected were the recumbent and flankers, as they required the greatest effort and care (in contrast to the rest of the circle stones which are often placed haphazardly). It has been suggested that at some sites these elements were the only ones ever erected, eg South Leylodge, NJ 766132 or Stonehead, NJ 600287. Although several recumbent stone circles contain low burial mounds called ring cairns, it is by no means certain that these circles were built primarily as funerary monuments.

Stonehead recumbent and flankers

Cup-marked stone at Balquhain

Aiky Brae: rituals would have taken place in the central space

the small egalitarian farming communities who co-operated to build the circles would have found helpful, other relevant rituals can be imagined in the central space. The fertility of crops and animals may have been ensured by acts of sympathetic or imitative magic performed within the bonfire-lit circle to urgent, entrancing drumming that faded into night's blackness all around.

The importance of the moon to the users of recumbent stone circles is emphasised by the cup-marks found at 12 central Grampian sites. They are precisely located, either on the recumbent (eg Sunhoney, no. 99; Rothiemay, NJ 550487) or the flankers or the stone adjacent (eg Loanhead, no. 98; Balquhain, NJ 735240). Recent research has shown that the cup-marks cluster at the point where the (major standstill) moon rises or sets: this last event is seen clearest at Cothiemuir Wood (NJ 617198) where there is a little group of cup-marks at the western end of the outer face of the recumbent.

A further link to the moon may be seen in the recurrent use of quartzite, either as complete blocks for the recumbent (Auchmaliddie, NJ 881448; North Strone, NJ 584138) or broken on site and scattered over the bank (Strichen, no. 93) or near the recumbent (Castle Fraser, NJ 714125). Whether the circle builders made the imaginative comparison between the gleaming milky whiteness of quartzite and moonlight cannot of course be proved.

Much has been written of the possible influences from other areas which might account for the development of the recumbent stone circle. The Clava cairns (passage graves and ring cairns with surrounding stone circles) of the Inverness area are certainly closely related, sharing an interest in south-south-western orientations, the grading of the stones of the circle, and the use of quartzite and cup-marks, and in having a mutually exclusive distribution, at least of the passage graves and recumbent stone circles. The practice of

Pyres may have been lit, and token cremations or dedicatory offerings may have been made initially, but the ring cairns probably represent a later use of these sites, perhaps many centuries after their erection. For example, excavation proved that the construction of the cairn at Loanhead of Daviot (no. 98) was the final identifiable act.

The initial use of the monument centred on the massive recumbent slab and its flanking pillars. These, it is now known, are arranged to frame the rising or setting of the (major standstill) moon in the southern sky, when viewed from inside the circle. It follows that for the monument to fulfil this primary function the centre would have had to be unencumbered by ring cairns. Furthermore, as such lunar observations can be used to define broad, seasonal, changes of a kind that

Lang Stane o'Craigearn

surrounding a chambered tomb with a stone circle was in fact extremely rare in the British Isles and Ireland. Apart from Clava, the Irish tombs on the Boyne, such as New Grange, are the only examples. Given that Grampian possesses not only large numbers of a fully developed and unique monument in its heartland (around Alford), but also examples of collateral types at Ballindalloch in the west of the region (Lagmore, no. 102; Marionburgh, no. 101; Dalmore, NJ 185308) and the related ring cairns of Raedykes (no. 89) and Clune Hill (NO 794949) to the SE, it can be argued that the influences flowed out from, rather than into, Grampian.

In summary, recumbent stone circles are seen as primarily communal, seasonal ritual centres, some of which were subsequently adapted to cremation burial. A related ritual monument of the later third or early second millennium of which there are a few examples in the region is the henge, a ceremonial enclosure defined usually by a circular earthen bank surrounding a ditch and central level space. That at Broomend of Crichie (no. 85) was the hub of an important ritual complex, now sadly damaged. The central grave found in the 19th century may indicate a move away from the community ethos of the earlier circles, while the fine stone battle axe of the second millennium carefully deposited in a pit within the circle-henge may represent an act of 'ritual desecration' similar to the placing of a wristguard fragment of beaker type in a pit within the recumbent stone circle at Candle Hill, Old Rayne (NJ 599299), or the deposition of beaker sherds, symbolic of the new craft of metalworking, at Loanhead of Daviot (no. 98), Old Keig (no. 97) or Berrybrae (NK 027571). All these deposits can be seen as final acts in the use of such sites, acts which may have challenged the old communal social order.

The stone circle tradition was so potent in Grampian, however, that it persisted in various forms throughout much of the second millennium. The two main features of the later monuments are their smaller size and comparative lack of regularity of form. The small stone settings at Glassel (no. 87), South Ythsie (NJ 884303) or Craighead (NO 911977) are typical of this development, one that ultimately reduced to the curious 'four poster' such as Templestone, Rafford (NJ 068569) or North Burreldales, Alvah (NJ 675549). The burial monument, the ring cairn, also reduces in size to the kerb cairn, such as the spectacular quartzite features at Logie Newton (no. 80). The two strands unite in the boulder circle at Cullerlie (no. 88), which encloses eight minute kerb cairns and in which the tenacious interest in the south-west still survives. There are also several impressive single standing stones in the region, such as the Lang Stane o'Craigearn at Kemnay (NJ 723149), the Candle Stane near Ellon (NJ 921348) or Camus's Stone, near Duffus (NJ 152682).

A major social contrast between the early beginnings of these 'circles of the moon' in the neolithic society of the third millennium and their end, in the later second millennium, can be seen at Loanhead of Daviot (no. 98). On the one hand, the awesome, communally created recumbent stone circle, in use for centuries for seasonal rites and, ultimately, for burial, and, on the other, the slight, unobtrusive, enclosed cremation cemetery used for a few years, or a generation or two at most, for the interment of small family groups of individuals.

85 Broomend of Crichie, Ceremonial Centre, Inverurie, Gordon

Later 3rd millennium BC.

NJ 779196. 2 km S of centre of Inverurie, in field beside A 96 (on broad bend of road just S of Port Elphinstone).

The now subdued circle-henge, 33.5 m from crest to crest of the banks, on a gravel terrace of the River Don, just downstream from its confluence with the Urie, is

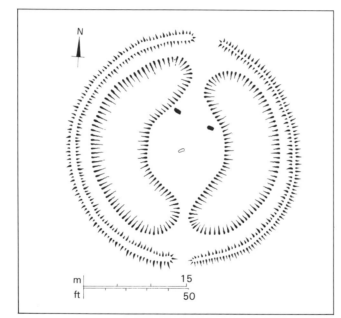

Broomend of Crichie (no. 85): henge from W

only one component of what was once a late neolithic ceremonial complex of considerable importance. The principal extant monument is the henge with entrances to north and south within which are two stones, the survivors of a six-stone concentric circle. (The stone at the centre is a fine Pictish symbol stone, with beast and crescent, of c AD 600, which was placed here for safety in the 19th century.) At the base of each stone were deposits of cremated bones, in pits or cists or cordoned urns. In 1855 three separate deposits were found in front of the north-western stone: a prestigious decorated sandstone battle axe, a small circular cist and a cordoned urn. In the centre of the circle was a shaft grave more than 1.9 m deep with, at the bottom, a cist containing a 'tolerably entire' skeleton and a deposit of cremated bones.

Some 50 m N of the circle-henge stood a large ring, 45.7 m in diameter, of three concentric circles of stones with a small cairn at their centre. The 1757 description mentions an 'altar of one stone, with a cavity in the upper part, wherein some of the blood of the sacrifice was put'. This may well have been a recumbent stone circle. It was destroyed by quarrying.

A great avenue of standing stones ran south from the destroyed site to the circle-henge and on for about 400 m to a spot close to the river. The avenue has been estimated as 18.3 m wide and to have contained 36 stones in each side, but only three remain, one of which can be seen just south of the henge.

In a sandbank a few metres to the west of the south end of the avenue, a small cemetery of four short cists was found in 1866. Two of the cists were larger than average and contained double burials covered with ox hides and accompanied by beakers (now in RMS). The cist cemetery and the battle axe have been interpreted as 'meaningful acts of desecration' of the old ceremonial centre by individuals or family groups who wished to demonstrate their newly acquired high status.

86 Wormy Hillock, Henge, Clashindarroch Forest, Gordon

Late 3rd millennium BC.
NJ 449307. 10 km S of Huntly; turn W off A 97 Huntly/Rhynie road c 4 km S of Huntly on minor road to Mytice. At road end follow track through trees (a walk of 2.5 km) to small burn and junction with another track; henge lies 50 m up burn.
Forestry Commission.

Although the location of this little ceremonial enclosure may seem remote to modern eyes, the gravel soils of the Rhynie area clearly attracted settlement from early times. The henge consists of a low circular bank, 16.5 m in diameter, with one entrance in the south-east which gives access across the shallow ditch to the level central area, a mere 6 m in diameter. The low-lying position of the henge, close to water, is typical, although few are so enclosed by the sides of a glen.

Glassel stone setting (no. 87)

87 Glassel, Stone Setting, Banchory, Kincardine and Deeside

2nd millennium BC.
NO 648996. 6 km NW of Banchory. Opposite entrance to Glassel House, on back road from Banchory to Torphins, walk down small ride through trees for c 100 m, turn left on small path for 100 m.

An oval setting of five granite pillars, 5.5 m by 2.8 m, the tallest on the south-west, situated on level ground at 110 m but near a sharp drop to the Canny Burn. The stones range in height from 0.84 m to 0.99 m. The site was dug into sometime before 1879 and re-excavated in 1904 when a small flint flake and a few charcoal fragments were found. The block of indurated sandstone lying loose may have been a cist cover.

This setting is similar to Image Wood, Aboyne (NO 524990) and the east circle at Backhill of Drachlaw (NJ 672463), transitional in form between recumbent stone circles of the third millennium and four-post stone settings of the later second millennium BC.

88 Standing Stones of Cullerlie, Echt, Gordon

2nd millennium BC.
NJ 785042. 15 km W of centre of Aberdeen. Turn S off B 9119 Aberdeen/Tarland road at Garlogie and in 250 m fork left; circle lies on left of road in 1 km.
HBM (SDD).

This manicured stone circle is set, unusually, on a ridge of gravel running into the low plain of Leuchar Moss at 90 m OD. Eight rough boulders, graded to the north and with their bases keeled, are set in a ring, 10.2 m in diameter, within which lie eight small kerb

149

cairns. The central cairn is the largest, at 3.4 m in diameter; it is the only one to have a double kerb. This and six other cairns each has 11 kerbstones.

Excavation in 1934 established that the site had first been levelled, the eight ring stones and the kerbs of the cairns erected; a fire of willow branches had then been lit amongst them. Cremated bone was deposited in seven of the kerb cairns and the cairns were infilled. The finding of oak charcoal in five cairns and hazel charcoal in one other cairn could indicate that not all the deposits were contemporary. Cairn 2, which lies to the west of the central cairn, contained a central, capstone-covered fire pit with lumps of charcoal and cremated human bone. The only objects found from the whole site were minute potsherds and three small worked flakes.

This setting is seen as a later development from the recumbent stone circle tradition.

Standing Stones of Cullerlie (no. 88)

Standing Stones of Cullerlie (no. 88): kerb cairn

89 Raedykes, Ring Cairns, Stonehaven, Kincardine and Deeside

3rd/2nd millennium BC.
NO 832906. 5.5 km NW of Stonehaven. Turn N off A 957 Stonehaven/Banchory road after crossing the Cowie Water; fork left almost immediately and in 1 km walk up track to West Raedykes and on to first cairn (1 km).

Strung along the crest of Campstone Hill at c 190 m OD, this important group of early ritual sites has open views to the east. The first feature, 280 m north-west of West Raedykes, is a fine ring cairn, 9.4 m in diameter and 0.4 m high, with the kerbed open central area, 3.9 m in diameter, clearly visible. Nine stones up to 1 m high survive in the surrounding

Raedykes (no. 89): ring cairn

Raedykes (no. 89): elaborated SW arc of ring cairn

stone circle, 17 m in diameter. 20 m to the west-north-west is an oval cairn, 8.5 m by 7.7 m and 0.5 m high, which is either a ring cairn or a robbed round cairn. The third site, 15 m further to the west-north-west, is very similar. The fourth feature stands higher than the others and 80 m north-west of the first; it comprises another ring cairn, 10.2 m in diameter and 0.6 m high, within a stone circle 13.9 m in diameter, of which five of the possible 13 stones remain. A close relationship with the recumbent stone circle tradition can be seen on the south-south-west arc of the cairn, where two tall stones are set close together (the western is 1.7 m and the eastern is 1.1 m tall) with the stump of another in between. Other pillar stones protrude at intervals from the kerb. This emphasis on the south-west was echoed in the surrounding stone circle.

90 Nine Stanes, Recumbent Stone Circle, Mulloch, Garrol Hill, Kincardine and Deeside

3rd/2nd millennium BC.

NO 723912. 4 km SE of Banchory. Turn W off A 957 (Slug Road) at Burn of Sheeoch bridge on to back road to Strachan; in 2.5 km enter woods to N of road; circle lies on right of track c 100 m to N of gate.

Forestry Commission.

Lichen covered and grey amongst the larches, this recumbent stone circle is in a classic position, on a hill shelf with broad views to the south and west. In plan, however, it differs from early circles like East Aquhorthies (no. 100), Sunhoney (no. 99) or Castle Fraser (NJ 714125) in being a 'flattened circle', 18 m by 14.6 m, with the mossy recumbent and flankers on the straighter side. One flanker has fallen but six other standing stones of medium height remain. The ring cairn within the circle runs against the squat recumbent, and still bears evidence of a 19th century 'excavation' which found cremated bone.

91 Tomnaverie, Recumbent Stone Circle, Tarland, Kincardine and Deeside

3rd/2nd millennium BC.

NJ 486034. 5 km NW of Aboyne; on B 9094, c 0.5 km E of its junction with A 974 Ballater/ Tarland road. Walk of 250 m up track to S. HBM (SDD).

Although part of the prominent little hill on which this recumbent stone circle sits has been removed by quarrying, the setting and the spectacular views south and west to the Cairngorms can still be appreciated. The recumbent, of whinstone, and four of the circle stones of pale red granite remain erect. The circle was about 18 m in diameter and it surrounded a ring cairn, 14 m across, whose substantial kerb still survives.

Nine Stanes, Mulloch (no. 90): recumbent and flankers

Tomnaverie recumbent stone circle (no. 91): kerb of ring cairn in foreground

92 Eslie the Greater, Recumbent Stone Circle, Banchory Ternan, Kincardine and Deeside

3rd millennium BC.
NO 717915. 4 km S of Banchory. Turn S off B 974 at Bridge of Feugh, fork right and in 2 km fork left. In 2.5 km turn right; circle is in field on right at top of brae.

This well-preserved recumbent stone circle stands at 180 m OD just below the crest of a low saddle with wide views to the south and west. Of the eight original circle stones (plus recumbent and flankers), five still stand; they range from 1.5 m to 0.8 m in height, the one opposite the recumbent being, characteristically,

Eslie the Greater recumbent stone circle (no. 92)

the smallest. In plan the circle is an ellipse, 26.5 m by 23.2 m. The enclosed ring cairn is 18 m in diameter with a clearly visible central space, 6.3 m in diameter; the cairn has been augmented by field gatherings. The recumbent, 2.9 m long, is slightly east of south, like other Deeside recumbent stone circles. Two lines of stones run from the ends of the recumbent to the perimeter of the ring cairn, creating a 'reserved area' similar to East Aquhorthies (no. 100) or Loanhead (no. 98).

The circle is intervisible with another, Eslie the Lesser, 0.8 km to the north-east (NO 722921), which is 15.3 m in diameter and is located on a shoulder 20 m higher than Eslie the Greater.

93 Strichen, Recumbent Stone Circle, Banff and Buchan

3rd/2nd millennium BC.
NJ 936544. 15 km NW of Peterhead. Turn off A 981 Fraserburgh/New Deer road 1.3 km S of Strichen and fork right in 250 m. Park on track to cottage and pass along right hand side of house and uphill for 400 m.

This recumbent stone circle, at 85 m OD, on a false crest below the summit of a rounded Buchan hill, reflects in its history of decay the landscape changes of the past two and a half centuries. When Dr Johnson visited it in 1773, the 'druidical circle' was in woodland; approximately 20 years later a tenant farmer pulled the stones down but was forced to re-erect them by order of the landowner. Recent excavation demonstrated that the circle was re-created to the south of the original site so that the recumbent appeared, anomalously, on the north arc of the new circle. This 're-creation' was itself bulldozed away in 1965. In 1979-83 the circle was excavated and restored in its original position; a visit is now a rewarding, prehistoric, experience.

Strichen recumbent stone circle (no. 93): the bank, typical of Buchan circles, can be seen

Loudon Wood recumbent stone circle (no. 94)

Strichen is a typical Buchan recumbent stone circle, with the stones sitting on a slight bank which forms a flattened circle, shorter north to south (12.1 m by 11 m). The recumbent is oriented on the extreme southern moon. One evocative discovery of the excavation was that the bank had been liberally covered with quartzite flakes, broken on site on an anvil stone.

94 Loudon Wood, Recumbent Stone Circle, Old Deer, Banff and Buchan
3rd millennium BC.
NJ 960497. 17 km W of Peterhead. Turn N off A 950 4 km W of Mintlaw, on to side road to Strichen. In c 0.5 km enter wood on right. Walk of c 1 km uphill (signposted).
Forestry Commission.

Positioned near the top of a long hill slope, its outlook masked until recently by mature, closely set conifers, this is a classic Buchan variant of the recumbent stone circle, having a bank, 0.8 m high, on to which the standing stones had been dragged and levered into position. Unlike Strichen (no. 93) but similar to Netherton (NK 043572) and Aiky Brae (NJ 958470), this is circular in plan, being 17.6 m in diameter. Although only the lichen-encrusted recumbent, west flanker and two other stones remain standing, this green, mossy, circle is still an unearthly spot. The 12-ton recumbent would have required at least 40 adults to pull it up the slope.

95 Tyrebagger, Recumbent Stone Circle, Dyce, Aberdeen

3rd/2nd millennium BC.
NJ 859132. Turn N off A 96 Aberdeen/Inverurie road at Chapel of Stoneywood. In 1 km go straight ahead on to track. 1.5 km uphill take third track on left to site.

Tyrebagger recumbent stone circle (no. 95)

Midmar Kirk recumbent stone circle (no. 96): paired flankers

Superbly sited on a hill shoulder at c 158 m OD, this recumbent stone circle is 18.3 m in diameter. The circle stones, from 1 m to 2.9 m tall, stand in a low stony bank surrounding a fragmentary ring cairn 11.6 m across. The characteristic differentiation between the recumbent and the circle stones can be seen here, the former being of dark grey granite (weighing 24 tons) and the latter a red, gritty granite from near at hand.

96 Midmar Kirk, Recumbent Stone Circle, Echt, Gordon

3rd millennium BC.
NJ 699064. 18 km W of centre of Aberdeen. 3.5 km W of Echt turn N off B 9119 Aberdeen/Tarland road (signposted Midmar Kirk); circle is in kirkyard 250 m up road.

This landscaped and re-arranged recumbent stone circle, 17.3 m in diameter, still impresses the traveller with two splendid flankers, each 2.5 m tall, which have been matched and shaped into two enormous canine teeth. The great recumbent is 4.5 m long and weighs 20 tons. It is likely that at least one stone, on the north-north-west, has been re-erected and the ring cairn tidied away, probably when the graveyard was laid out around the circle in 1914.

97 Old Keig, Recumbent Stone Circle, Keig, Gordon

3rd millennium BC.
NJ 596193. 3 km NNE of Alford. Turn NW off B 992 Insch/Whitehouse road at Keig crossroads; at top of brae, in c 2 km, park at old quarry and walk down shelter belt opposite for 300 m.

At once communal and anonymous, the essentially neolithic nature of the recumbent stone circle is perhaps nowhere better seen than at Old Keig where the circle, 20 m in diameter, is now represented by a gigantic recumbent of sillimanite gneiss, two flankers and one other stone, standing on a low bank. The circle is located on a very slight crest on rising ground with distant, sometimes magical, views over the Howe of Alford. The site was probably levelled and the enormous recumbent, which weighs 53 tons and is the largest known (4.9 m by 2.1 m by 2.0 m), dragged from somewhere in the Don valley about 10 km away. The last 1 km would have been uphill, at a gradient of 1:14, requiring well over 100 people. Prior to the building of the eccentrically placed ring cairn, a small timber structure may have stood for a short time in the central area (cf Loanhead, no. 98).

Old Keig (no. 97): the massive recumbent

98 Loanhead of Daviot, Recumbent Stone Circle, Daviot, Gordon

3rd/2nd millennia BC.
NJ 747288. 7 km N of Inverurie; between the A 920 Oldmeldrum/Colpy and B 9001 Inverurie/ Rothienorman roads; signposted.
HBM (SDD).

A recumbent stone circle, 20.5 m in diameter, of eight standing stones, two flankers and a massive, frost-split recumbent, crouching on a broad shelf at 155 m OD, near the summit of a gentle hill. The stones of the circle are graded in height and the one immediately east of the east flanker has a vertical line of five cup-marks on its inner face (another seven have been claimed on this stone). Each stone stood in a little cairn, beneath which was a pit containing charcoal and pottery shreds. The central ring cairn, with its prominent kerb, occupies most of the interior of the circle. It overlay traces of burning which, in the central space, included sherds, charcoal, human cremated bone (children's skull fragments and adult bones) and retouched flint flakes. It is possible that a small rectangular timber mortuary house (1.2 m by 0.6 m) was represented by four shallow holes in the very middle of the central space. An arc of kerbing reserves a space in front of the 12-ton recumbent, which is skewed into the circle. From the pottery found here it is likely that the use of the circle extended over many centuries and that it fell out of use during the beaker period (c 2000 BC).

The two arcs of low stone walling, with entrances at the west and east, that lie immediately south-east of the circle comprise an enclosed cremation cemetery of the bronze age. Excavation in 1935 revealed a burial in a shallow central scoop, consisting of the partially incinerated remains of a 40 year-old man. The pyre had been placed over the body and, unusually, the partially cremated remains had not been gathered up but rather the area had been used for subsequent cremations. An adjacent, empty, pit may have been

Loanhead of Daviot (no. 98):
recumbent stone circle and enclosed
cremation cemetery

used for the storage of bodies before cremation. To the north-east and south more burial deposits were found, 11 in urns and the rest in pits.

Whereas the great stone circle had required the co-operation of a whole community (and their neighbours) to build it, and while its use for the rituals of life, fertility and magic extended over many centuries, the cremation cemetery is an altogether slighter, more transient creation, concerned with the relationships in death within an individual family or two over a short time.

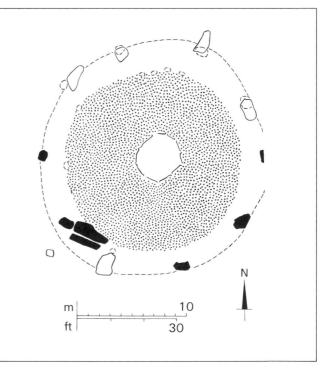

Loanhead of Daviot recumbent
stone circle (no. 98): plan

Loanhead of Daviot (no. 98):
recumbent and flankers

157

99 Sunhoney, Recumbent Stone Circle, Echt, Gordon

3rd/2nd millennium BC.
NJ 715056. 22 km W of centre of Aberdeen. Turn N off B 9119 Aberdeen/Tarland road c 2 km W of Echt. Walk up past farm and along field edge to W to tree clump (180 m).

A fine recumbent stone circle, 25.4 m in diameter, consisting of a recumbent, two flanking pillars and nine other standing stones, located on a well defined but low hill shoulder at 125 m OD. The recumbent has slumped and part of it has broken off; it bears 31 cup-marks. It is a fine-grained grey granite whereas all the other stones are a reddish granite or a gneiss. Traces of a low ring cairn can be seen in the interior. Charles Elphinstone Dalrymple dug into the ring in 1865 and found deposits of cremated bone and some fire-marked stones in the central space. A 'circular' cist with some fragments of a 'rude stone vessel' lay at the south side of the ring cairn. As at Loanhead of Daviot (no. 98), each circle stone stood in a little low cairn, although today the stones appear to be in a low bank; the circle may have undergone some restoration. The recumbent is aligned on the point at which the moonrise is first visible above the hills to the south. The circular plan of Sunhoney places it early in the development of such circles.

Sunhoney recumbent stone circle (no. 99): cup-marks on the fallen recumbent

Easter Aquhorthies recumbent stone circle (no. 100)

100 Easter Aquhorthies, Recumbent Stone Circle, Inverurie, Gordon

3rd millennium BC.
NJ 732207. 3 km W of Inverurie. In centre of Inverurie, turn W off A 96 (signposted) along Blackhall Road. At junction outside Inverurie carry straight on up hill. Park at top and walk up lane to left and take first right.
HBM (SDD).

An impressive recumbent stone circle, 19.5 m in diameter, consisting of nine erect stones, the recumbent, two flankers and, in addition, two massive blocks which form a reserved area in front of the recumbent (cf Loanhead, no. 98; Eslie, no. 92). The circle is located near the crest of a hill shoulder, at 175 m OD. The characteristic differentiation between the recumbent with its flankers and the other circle stones can be seen vividly, both in terms of height of stones and their geological origin. The stones are graded in height from the 2.25 m tall flankers to the 1.7 m high stones on the circumference opposite, and, while the nine circle stones are of rough pinkish porphyry or (in the case of the stone next to the east flanker) a glowing red jasper, the flankers are of grey granite and the recumbent of reddish granite from near Bennachie. The outer face of the 3.8 m long recumbent has been smoothed carefully. The circle stones are set in a low bank which has been partly augmented in recent times. The very slight rise in the interior and a 1934 reference to a cist suggest the existence of a later ring cairn, now vestigial. Its almost perfectly circular plan places this circle early in the series of recumbent stone circles.

101 Marionburgh, Clava Cairn, Ballindalloch, Moray

3rd millennium BC.
NJ 183364. 10 km SW of Aberlour. Turn W off
A 95 Craigellachie/Grantown road opposite
entrance to Marionburgh down a broad track for
170 m. Cairn in walled enclosure on S side.

Standing at 190 m OD on a terrace above the River
Avon, near its confluence with the Spey, are five stones
of a circle, 23.9 m in diameter, of which the stone in
the south-west is a lofty 2.74 m tall. Within is a ring
cairn comprising a circular bank of small stones, about
14 m in diameter with a central space 5 m in diameter.

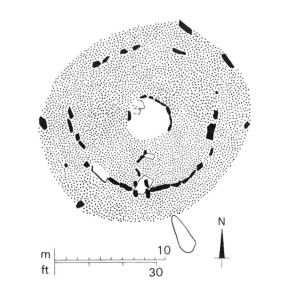

Lagmore Clava cairn (no. 102): plan

102 Lagmore West, Clava Cairn, Ballindalloch, Moray

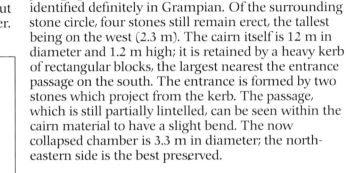

3rd millennium BC.
NJ 176358. 11 km SW of Aberlour. Turn S off
A 95 Craigellachie/Grantown road immediately E
of its junction with the B 9137; in 100 m stop at
layby and walk up through fields to W to
shoulder of hill (130 m).

Dramatically sited at 195 m OD, high above the
confluence of the Spey and the Avon, this is the only
passage grave of the Clava tradition to have been
identified definitely in Grampian. Of the surrounding
stone circle, four stones still remain erect, the tallest
being on the west (2.3 m). The cairn itself is 12 m in
diameter and 1.2 m high; it is retained by a heavy kerb
of rectangular blocks, the largest nearest the entrance
passage on the south. The entrance is formed by two
stones which project from the kerb. The passage,
which is still partially lintelled, can be seen within the
cairn material to have a slight bend. The now
collapsed chamber is 3.3 m in diameter; the north-
eastern side is the best preserved.

300 m to the east and c 35 m below this site, is another
similar but heavily damaged feature, adjacent to the
main road, at NJ 179359. One of the fallen stones to its
north-east bears many cup-marks.

TOMBS OF THE ANCESTORS

The earliest tombs built by the first farmers in the north-east survive as elongated, wedge-shaped, trapezoidal or oval earthen mounds or cairns of stone. Two distinct types of location were chosen. One was conspicuous hilltop or skyline locations, in which the cairn would have been visible not only to the community that constructed it, living and working on the hillslopes around, but also to more distant communities in neighbouring valleys, or even, in some cases, to anyone approaching from the sea. The large and prominent cairns such as Gourdon (no. 105), Cairn Catto (no. 103), Woods of Finzean (NO 591937), Longmanhill (NJ 737620), or Cairnborrow (NJ 453414) may thus have performed as territorial markers as well as the resting places of a select band of the community's ancestors. The other location favoured was the edges of less elevated terraces such as at Midmill (no. 107), Capo (no. 106), Blackhill Wood (NO 796817), West Hatton (NJ 851070) or Pitlurg (NK 024336).

Some variations in the plans of these long burial mounds, such as the separation of one end by a difference in height, a dip in the profile, or a constriction in the plan (eg Balnagowan, no. 104; Longmanhill) may indicate that these are composite monuments, adapted or added to over many generations. So little excavation has been carried out on them that it is not possible to say if any of them cover burial chambers. Certainly, the slighter earthen ones probably do not (eg Capo, no. 106; Pitlurg). However, the huge scale of some of the others, particularly some of the hilltop examples such as Woods of Finzean, Longmanhill or Balnagowan (no. 104), means that the possibility should not be excluded.

What is clear is the amount of toil and resources that the early farmers were prepared to expend on erecting monuments to their ancestors. Even such comparatively modest long mounds as the (now destroyed) barrow at Dalladies, Kincardine and Deeside, required 6000 man hours and 0.73 ha of turf.

The distinctive profile of the Longmanhill cairn.

103 Cairn Catto, Long Cairn, Longside, Banff and Buchan

4th/3rd millennium BC.
NK 074421. 6.5 km SW of Peterhead. Cairn lies immediately W of minor road linking A 952 Ellon/Peterhead and A 950 Peterhead/New Pitsligo roads and beside a field boundary that runs at right angles to the road just S of Hill of Dens.

Although the plan of this great wedge-shaped long cairn is rather disturbed, it is still an important feature of the Buchan landscape, lying at 80 m OD in very open, rolling country. The cairn is built of many heavy stones, still bare, and is aligned NW–SE. It is 48 m long and higher and wider at the rounded south-eastern end, which is 22 m across and 1.8 m high.

Cairn Catto long cairn (no. 103)

Balnagowan long cairn (no. 104): plan

104 The Blue Cairn of Balnagowan, Long Cairn, Tarland, Kincardine and Deeside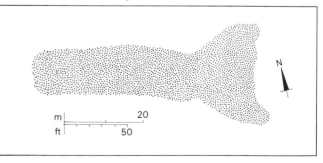

4th/3rd millennium BC.
NJ 490005. 3 km NW of Aboyne; on B 9094 Aboyne/Tarland road, turn W on to track just S of Mill of Gellan. Walk up track for 1 km to Muir Cottage, turn right (W) and climb through rough pasture (gates/stock) to saddle between Balnagowan Hill and Craig Dhu.

This magnificent long cairn, apparently unchambered, stands at 244 m OD, just below the crest of a saddle between two prominent hills in the centre of the Howe of Cromar, with a view to the north. It is thus at the hub of one of the areas of greatest interest to the first farmers, who settled these gentle slopes nearly 6000 years ago. The great cairn of grey bare boulders is 53.3 m long, 18.3 m wide and a maximum of 1.8 m high. Its long axis is ESE–WNW. At the east end is a wide, shallow forecourt, defined by two horns, from 0.31 m to 0.61 m high, which project about 3 m beyond the main body of the cairn. 12 m from the east end there is a distinct hollow in the cairn material, which corresponds to the pronounced 'waist' or constriction that is visible in plan. There is therefore the possibility that this is a two-stage monument, similar to Longmanhill near Banff (NJ 737620). The Balnagowan cairn is intervisible with one on the hillside to the west, at Belnacraig (NJ 478008). (See also no. 79 for a field system.)

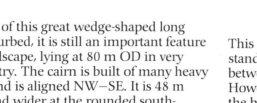

m   20
ft   50

N

105 Gourdon, Long Cairn, Gourdon, Kincardine and Deeside

4th/3rd millennium BC.
NO 818706. 3 km S of Inverbervie turn W off A 92 to Nether Benholm then turn right uphill to cairn which is on the hill summit c 90 m SE of the track.

This long cairn, now turf-covered, is conspicuously sited at 136 m OD on a hilltop overlooking the sea. It is oriented ENE–WSW and is 46 m long and 14 m wide at the east end. The east end is the higher (1.7 m) and, like the west end, is rounded in plan; the cairn material includes rounded boulders and some earth.

106 Capo, Long Barrow, Inglismaldie Forest, Kincardine and Deeside

4th/3rd millennium BC.
NO 633664. 8 km SW of Laurencekirk on minor road to Edzell, between A 94 and B 966. 1.3 km NW of A 94 turn W on to forest track. A walk of 500 m (taking the left fork) leads to the barrow. Forestry Commission.

This is a rare survival of an important type of neolithic monument, the earthen long barrow. Composed of scraped-up turf and earth, it appears to be intact. It is located on the edge of a low terrace above the river North Esk, and is 80 m long, 28 m wide at the east end and 2.5 m high. A very similar example was excavated (and subsequently removed in gravel quarrying) in 1971 at Dalladies, about 1.1 km to the north.

Capo long barrow (no. 106)

Midmill long cairn (no. 107)

107 Midmill, Long Cairn, Kintore, Gordon

4th/3rd millennium BC.
NJ 795151. 1 km S of Kintore; pull off A 96 at Midmill depot and walk E along field boundary for 300 m.

This substantial long cairn, now turf- and whin-covered, occupies a rounded crest on the end of a broad, low ridge above a dry valley in the heart of the Garioch. The cairn is oriented east-west and has been mutilated by quarrying at its east end. Nevertheless, the surviving remains are still impressive, if simple in plan, about 72 m long, 26 m wide and up to 3 m high.

Bronze statue of Wallace and
His Majesty's Theatre, Aberdeen.

MUSEUMS

The principal museums in Aberdeen are:

Anthropological Museum, University of Aberdeen
Marischal College, Broad Street.
Extensive local collections, including a
reconstruction of a short cist burial,
and an excellent modern
anthropological display.

Art Gallery and Museum, Schoolhill (This, and the
following three museums are run by
the City of Aberdeen District Council.)
Fine permanent collection.

James Dun's House, Schoolhill.
Temporary exhibitions and cist
reconstruction.

Provost Skene's House, Guestrow.
A fine 16th century town house with
important painted ceiling; houses
domestic items and an archaeological
display.

Maritime Museum, Provost Ross's House, Shiprow.
This well preserved 16th century town
house has been leased by the National
Trust for Scotland to the City of
Aberdeen who have established
comprehensive displays on

Grampian's maritime past and
present.

Outside Aberdeen, there are good local museums at:

Peterhead, run by North-East of Scotland Museums'
Service (NESMS), the Arbuthnott
Museum, St Peter's Street, has a wide
local collection; it is particularly noted
for its displays on the granite industry
and whaling.

Inverurie (NESMS), above the library in the Market
Place, has important collections of
local archaeological material.

Huntly (NESMS), in the Brander Library in the Square,
a small local history display.

Elgin, run by the Moray Society, the Museum at
1 High Street has many important
archaeological objects as well as
collections of natural history and
geology.

Forres, run by Moray District Council, the Museum in
the High Street has a wide collection
of local history and archaeology.

Burghead, run by Moray District Council, the small
museum in the library in Grant Street

contains several important objects from the promontory fort.

There are also small museums open during the summer, at:

Banff (NESMS, 25 High Street)
Banchory (NESMS, The Square)
Stonehaven (NESMS, Tolbooth, Harbour)
Dufftown (Moray District Council, The Square)
Keith (Moray District Council, Church Street).

In addition, there are displays dedicated to particular themes such as:

Farming History

Aden Country Park (see no. 4)
Pitmedden Garden (see no. 18)
Fasque House (see no. 1)
Tearie Visitors' Centre, Darnaway, Moray
Tomintoul (reconstructed blacksmith's forge in Square)

Fishing

Buckie (Town House West, Cluny Place)
Lossiemouth Fisheries and Community Museum (Pitgaveny Street)
Tugnet Icehouse (see no. 10)

Transport

Grampian Transport Museum, Alford.

Finally, the Royal Museum of Scotland, Queen Street, Edinburgh, has several important items from Grampian, such as the Celtic war-trumpet from Deskford, in its collections.

EXCURSIONS

Note: Access to the interiors of certain properties in the care of the National Trust for Scotland or the Historic Buildings and Monuments Directorate is limited to the months between May and September.
Furthermore the NTS houses are generally open only in the afternoons; visitors are advised to check on opening times.

Midmar and Lower Deeside

Leave Aberdeen by the A 944 road to Alford. At Kingswells, 3 km from the outskirts of Aberdeen, turn right (N) to visit the Consumption Dykes (no. 6). Return to the main road, turn right and in c 1 km turn right (N) again to view the West Hatton long cairn (NJ 851070). Return to main road, turn right, then fork

left on Tarland road (B 9119). In 6 km fork left again on Banchory road (B 9125) and in 300 m turn left for Cullerlie stone circle (no. 88).

(For a shorter tour, proceed S to Drum Castle (no. 31) and return to Aberdeen by A 93, viewing the cairn at West Cults (NJ 883028), off Quarry Road.)

Alternatively, return N to Echt road (B 9119) and turn left (W), passing the bulk of Barmekin of Echt with its multivallate hillfort (NJ 726071). In 6 km is Sunhoney recumbent stone circle (no. 99). Proceeding westwards, the towers of the 16th century Midmar Castle, a private home, can be glimpsed through the trees. To the S of the road are the old kirk of Midmar and the castle mound or motte of Cunningar (NJ 700059).

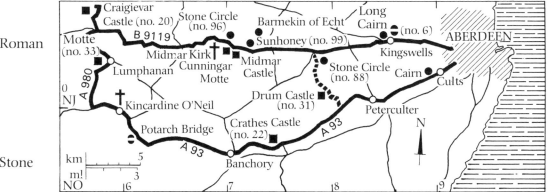

● Prehistoric and Roman
■ Castle
† Ecclesiastical
▲ Domestic
⬟ Industrial
▮ Pictish Symbol Stone
⬒ Miscellaneous

Turn right (N) off the road in c 400 m for Midmar Kirk recumbent stone circle (no. 96) in the modern graveyard.

Return to main road and travel W for 13 km, to Crossroads. Turn right (N: signposted) for Craigievar Castle (no. 20). After Craigievar, head S to the motte at Lumphanan (no. 33), then carry on southwards by Muir of Dess to Kincardine O'Neil, whose old kirk has a fine 14th century doorway (NO 592996). Head E

along A 93, passing Potarch bridge (1814) at NO 607973), to Banchory and on to Crathes Castle (no. 22). Return to Aberdeen via Drum Castle (no. 31), if time permits.

Formartine and Fyvie

Leave Aberdeen on A 947 Banff road; on north side of Dyce follow directions in entry no. 61 to view the Pictish stones at Chapel of St Fergus. On returning note the remains of the Aberdeenshire Canal to the left of the railway bridge beside the quarry. Proceed N up A 947; in 12 km turn left (W) on minor road, pass through Kirktown of Bourtie (NJ 804248) with its little kirk of 1806 and interesting graveyard: there is a Pictish stone fragment set high on the south wall of the kirk, at the east end. Pass the remains of a recumbent stone circle in the field to the N (NJ 800248). At the main road turn right (N) and in 0.5 km park at side of road (beside the 17th century Barra Castle, a private home) and climb Hill of Barra (no. 76) to the fort with wide views over the Garioch (a round trip of c 2.8 km).

Proceed N through Oldmeldrum to Fyvie Castle (no. 23), taking a detour to see the excellent farm-steading from the age of improvement at Bethelnie (NJ 784304). Fyvie kirkyard, with its Pictish stones, elaborate Gordon tombs (one with a phoenix and a pastiche of Ovid), the Leith enclosure and the grave of Bonnie Annie, is also worth a visit. Head S on back roads to A 920, to the S of which lies the recumbent stone circle of Loanhead of Daviot (no. 98). Return to Aberdeen via Inverurie, detouring to see the Harlaw Memorial at NJ 751240, and, at the N end of Inverurie, the Brandsbutt stone (no. 63), and, at the S end (in cemetery), the Bass of Inverurie (a motte) and three Pictish stones.

If time permits, make a detour to Kinkell church (no. 52) and return to the A 96 for the henge at Broomend of Crichie (no. 85), the Kintore symbol stone (no. 66)

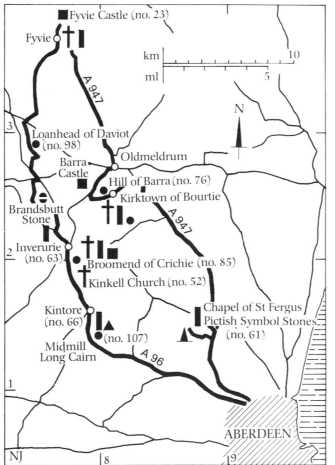

and fine town house, and the Midmill long cairn (no. 107).

The Garioch and Mid Donside

Leave Aberdeen by A 96 Inverurie road and, c 1 km W of turning for airport, turn right (N) off road (at trailer works) for Tyrebagger recumbent stone circle (no. 95). Return to A 96 and proceed to Kintore, passing the Midmill long cairn (no. 107) on the right c 1 km S of the town. In the centre of Kintore visit the symbol stone (no. 66) and view the fine town house. Go on to Inverurie, passing the henge at Broomend of Crichie (no. 85). In the centre of Inverurie fork left along Blackhall Road and follow signs for Easter Aquhorthies recumbent stone circle (no. 100).

Return down track and turn left (N) on back road past Balquhain Castle (NJ 731236) to Chapel of Garioch

and on to the Maiden Stone (no. 62). The active may then climb Bennachie by forking left for the car park.

Alternatively, proceed by way of the A 96 and the B 9002 to Insch, passing, just after leaving the A 96, the well-restored Harthill Castle (NJ 686251), a typical Aberdeenshire tower-house of the 16th century. Pass through Insch and follow signs to the Picardy Stone (no. 67). To climb to the fort on Dunnideer (no. 75), return to Insch and turn right; otherwise head SW on back road to Leslie, turn left (E) to pass the 17th century Leslie Castle (NJ 599248), now restored. At Auchleven, turn right (S) to skirt the Bennachie range and on to the Old Keig recumbent stone circle (no. 97).

Follow the Don down by the Lord's Throat, passing the Cothiemuir recumbent stone circle on its wooded hilltop (NJ 617198) and Pitfichie Castle (NJ 677166), arriving at the little planned village of Monymusk with its fine Norman church (no. 55). Proceed S to Cluny

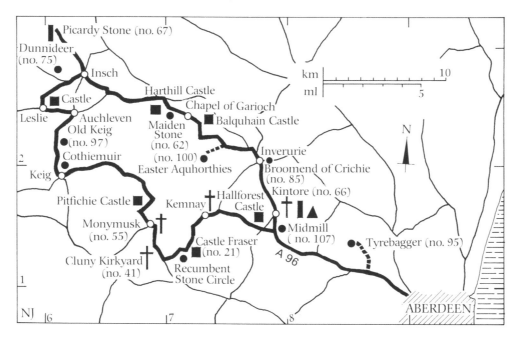

kirkyard (no. 41) then E by back roads to Castle Fraser (no. 21). (A fine recumbent stone circle with outliers can be seen by making a small detour to NJ 714125.) Finally, head for Kemnay, passing the Lang Stane o'Craigearn on a low hill behind the bungalow at the road junction (NJ 723149), and the Kemnay burial vault (NJ 737161). Pass the lofty remains of the early 14th century Hallforest Castle at NJ 777154 and return to Aberdeen on the A 96.

Kincardine

Leave Aberdeen by A 93 Banchory road. At Drumoak, 4 km W of Peterculter, turn left (S) and cross the fine iron double-span Park Bridge of 1854 (NO 796981). On reaching the south Deeside road (B 9077), turn right (W) and pass Durris motte (NO 779968) and Kirkton of Durris. Cross the A 957 and continue along Dee to Balbridie Farm; 400 m to the W on a small knoll to the N of the road is the site of the neolithic timber hall of Balbridie (NO 733959). Proceed westwards and take the first left on to Slug Road. In c 3 km turn right past Quithelhead then right, then at crossroads left for the stone circles of Eslie the Lesser (NO 722921), Eslie the Greater (no. 92) and the Nine Stanes, Mulloch (no. 90). Rejoin the A 957 and turn right (S) for Stonehaven. (The active may detour N at Rickarton to climb to the cairns at West Raedykes (no. 89) and the Roman camp (no. 68).) In Stonehaven visit the harbour with its museum in the old Tolbooth.

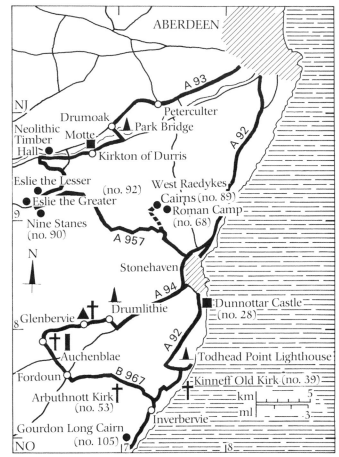

Leave Stonehaven by the coast road (A 92) and in 2 km visit Dunnottar Castle (no. 28). Proceed southwards on A 92, detouring to Todhead Point lighthouse (NO 869769). Carry on S by back roads to Kinneff Old Kirk (no. 39). Return to A 92 and pass through Inverbervie; in 2.5 km turn right (W) off road to Nether Benholm and up track to N to Gourdon long cairn (no. 105). Return to A 92, head N back through Inverbervie and after crossing bridge fork left on B 967 for Arbuthnott Kirk (no. 53) down side road to left in 2 km.

Proceed westwards to Fordoun, cross A 94 and head NW to Auchenblae. St Palladius's Chapel is on a knoll at the south end of the village (NO 726784) and the Pictish stone is in the present kirk (key at manse). Pass up the steep High Street and turn right for Glenbervie, where there is a (private) house largely of the 17th century and a kirkyard with graves of the ancestors of the poet Burns. Carry on to Drumlithie with its weavers' bell tower (NO 786809); join the A 94 E of Drumlithie and turn left (N) for Aberdeen.

Deeside and Strathdon

(Travellers prepared for a long day could begin by heading W from Ballater on the A 93 to Crathie Kirk (no. 35), Balmoral Bridge (no. 14) and the grounds of Balmoral Castle, if open. They should then take the old military road (B 976) N to Gairnshiel Bridge on the A 939.)

Leave Ballater on the A 939 and in 8 km cross Gairnshiel Bridge (NJ 294008), a fine piece of 18th century military engineering. Continue on A 939 and note where the old military road leaves the present road line in c 6 km at NJ 296063. Proceed to Corgarff Castle (no. 25), then turn E to follow the Don on the A 939, B 973 and A 97 to the Doune of Invernochty (no. 34) and on to Glenbuchat Castle (no. 24) and Kildrummy Castle (no. 30). The little kirk of

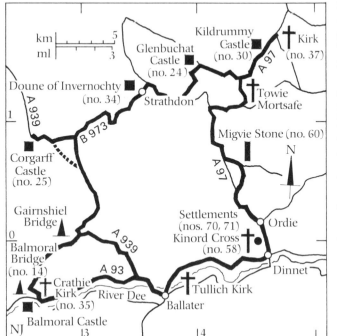

Kildrummy (no. 37) lies on a side road on the right, 2 km further N up the A 97. Retrace 5 km of the A 97 and at Glenkindie turn left (S) on side road to Towie (NJ 439129) to see the mortsafe in the kirkyard. Proceed along side roads to rejoin A 97 and travel S into Howe of Cromar. Once over watershed turn left (E) for Migvie Stone (no. 60) in kirkyard to N of side road, then head S to Logie Coldstone and Ordie. Enter Muir of Dinnet National Nature Reserve 1.5 km S of Ordie to view the settlements of New and Old Kinord (nos 70, 71) and the Kinord Cross (no. 58). Return to Ballater via Dinnet and A 93, passing, 2 km from Ballater, the ancient Christian site of Tullich Kirk (NO 390975) with its Pictish stone fragment.

Howe of Cromar

Begin at the site of the early castle of enclosure at Coull (NO 512022), to the south of the kirk on a side road off the B 9094 and 4 km N of Aboyne. Travel N on side road to join B 9119, turn left (W) and in 2 km stop at Culsh souterrain (no. 69). Proceed through Tarland and turn left on B 9094 for Tomnaverie recumbent stone circle (no. 91); return to Tarland and fork left then right for Migvie kirkyard with its Pictish stone (no. 60). Carry on to A 97, turn left (S). In 5.5 km fork left for Ordie and in 1.5 km enter Muir of Dinnet National Nature Reserve to visit settlements of New and Old Kinord (nos 70, 71) and the Kinord Cross (no. 58).

The Whisky Trail

This excursion follows part of the Whisky Trail, a signposted route round six malt whisky distilleries which are open to the public (check times locally).

The Glenfiddich Distillery (no. 9) and Balvenie Castle (no. 29), both at the N end of Dufftown, provide a convenient starting point. Visitors should then travel S through the centre of the planned village of Dufftown to the Kirkton of Mortlach (no. 56). A drive

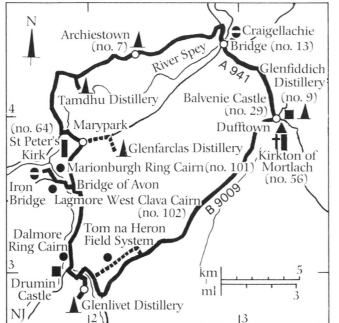

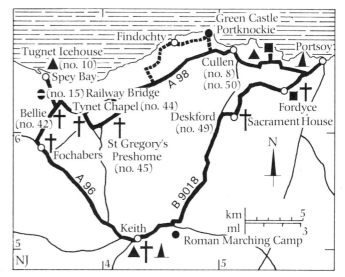

narrow road to the left, past Inveravon School, runs down to St Peter's kirk with its four Pictish symbol stones (no. 64).

At Marypark, c 1.5 km further N on the A 95, before turning left (W) to cross the Spey, a detour to the E of c 1.5 km takes in the Glenfarclas Distillery (NJ 211382). After crossing the Spey on the B 9138, turn right (N) on B 9102 to Tamdhu distillery (NJ 189418) whose visitors' centre uses the old station buildings. Return to the B 9102 for the little planned village of Archiestown (no. 7) and on to recross the Spey at Craigellachie and to view Telford's Craigellachie bridge (no. 13). The A 941 leads back to Dufftown.

North-eastern Moray

Beginning in Cullen (no. 8), the Square, Seatown, Harbour and motte (Castle Hill) can all be visited on foot. The old Kirk (no. 50) is best reached by car. Thereafter, take the coast road (A 98) to Portsoy, diverting to the N to see a good 16th century dovecote

southwestwards on the B 9009 through Glen Rinnes passes a side road from which the field system of Tom na Heron may be reached by the active (NJ 207313). The Glenlivet Distillery, where legal distilling began, lies to the S of the B 9136 near the confluence of the Livet and the Avon (NJ 195290).

A small detour of 1.5 km NW along the B 9136 passes Drumin Castle (NJ 184303); the route then follows the B 9008 northwards past the Dalmore ring cairn (NJ 185308) to Bridge of Avon, at the confluence of the Avon and the Spey. Here, high on a shelf to the S of the A 95, is the Lagmore West Clava cairn (no. 102). A minor road, the B 9137, runs N from the A 95 to Ballindalloch Station, from which the Speyside Way crosses the Spey on an impressive iron bridge of 1863 (NJ 168368). Return to Bridge of Avon and turn left (N); in 1 km a lane on the left leads to the Marionburgh ring cairn (no. 101). One km further N a and (for the intrepid) the exposed cliff site of Findlater Castle (NJ 541672), passing the disused windmill at Glenglassaugh (NJ 560657). In Portsoy walk around the old harbour and adjoining streets.

Go back along the A 98 for 1.5 km and turn left (S) for the tiny village of Fordyce with its 16th century tower and old kirkyard (NJ 555638). Continue W on side roads to Deskford Sacrament House (no. 49) in the old kirk.

Head S on B 9018 and in 10 km turn right on to A 95 at Auchinhove, the site of a Roman marching camp (NJ 462517). In Keith, visit the old bridge of 1609, the fragment of the tower of Milton Keith (c 1480), the old kirk, St Thomas's Roman Catholic church and Holy Trinity Episcopal church. The planned village of New Keith, founded by the earl of Fife in 1817, and the Strathisla Distillery may also be visited.

From Keith travel up the A 96 to Fochabers, whose square with classical church is particularly graceful. At the W end of the town turn right (N) off the A 96 on the B 9104 to Spey Bay. In c 1.7 km turn right for Bellie kirkyard (no. 42). Continue N to Tugnet Icehouse (no. 10) at Spey Bay. Approximately 1 km S

of Spey Bay to the right (W) of the road is a small carpark which gives access to the great Spey railway bridge (no. 15).

Proceed S through Bogmoor and turn left for Tynet Chapel (no. 44). Cross main road (A 98) and pass through Clochan to reach St Gregory's, Preshome (no. 45). Return to Cullen either by the A 98 or divert N to the fishing villages of Findochty and Portknockie; at the latter the small promontory fort of Green Castle may be seen to the E of the harbour (NJ 488687).

The Laich of Moray

Leave Elgin by the A 941 Rothes road; at the top of the hill in New Elgin turn right for Birnie Kirk (no. 57), then proceed across the Lossie and by back roads to Pluscarden Abbey (no. 46). Continue through Rafford, with its fine Gothic-revival church of 1826 by Gillespie Graham; turn right to pass the Templestone stone setting (NJ 068569, behind bungalows) and the remains of the 16th century Blervie Castle (NJ 070571). Turn left for Forres and visit the museum, Dallas Dhu Distillery (NJ 035565, 1 km S of Forres) and Sueno's Stone (no. 59).

Those prepared for a long day out could carry on westwards to Darnaway (Tearie Visitor Centre, NH 988569), Brodie Castle (no. 19) and Dyke kirk (NH 990584) before rejoining this excursion at Sueno's Stone at the east end of Forres.

From Sueno's Stone continue on B 9011 and B 9089 past the fragmentary remains of the Abbey of Kinloss (NJ 065615) and on to Burghead (no. 72). Then take the coast road through Hopeman and turn right for Duffus and St Peter's Kirk (no. 51) and the castle (no. 32). On leaving the castle turn left and left again for Quarrywood (Spynie) Kirk (NJ 182642). Return to Elgin via Spynie Palace (NJ 230658) which is undergoing consolidation but which can be viewed from the outside.

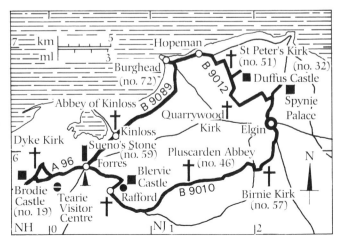

The Banff Coast

Begin in Banff with a visit to Duff House (no. 2), then head E along the coast on the A 98 through the fishing and boat-building town of Macduff. One km E of Macduff, fork left on the B 9031 and in 3.5 km note the prominent round cairn of Law of Melrose on the skyline to the N (NJ 757642). In another 4 km turn left (N) on the B 9123 to Gardenstown, founded in 1720 by Alexander Garden of Troup. Return to the B 9031, turn left and in 4 km, just before the deep den of the Tore of Troup, turn left on a track to a small carpark for the promontory fort of Castle Point (no. 73).

Proceed along the B 9031, diverting, if inclined, to the picturesque cliff-girt village of Pennan. Just before reaching New Aberdour, turn left for Aberdour beach on the west side of which are the old church of St Drostan's with two good 16th century recess tombs and an interesting pyramidal dovecote (NJ 884643). Carry on along the back road to Rosehearty, at the E end of which are the remains of the Dower House of 1573. Turn right (S) on a back road for the substantial ruins of the 15th century tower and 17th century pleasance of Pitsligo Castle (NJ 937669) and the kirk

with its heraldic laird's loft at NJ 933662. Turn left (E) at the junction and head for Fraserburgh, detouring by Sandhaven for the meal mill at its E end. In the substantial town of Fraserburgh, are the Kinnaird Head lighthouse (no. 16) and nearby Wine Tower, the 18th century mercat cross and 19th century town house and an extensive harbour.

Leave Fraserburgh by the A 981 Strichen road and in 4 km turn right (E) for the cairn of Memsie (no. 81). Return up the B 9032, cross the A 981 and in 4 km turn left (SW) on the A 98. In 1.5 km visit Tyrie kirk to see the Pictish stone with eagle beside the vestry (key at manse) (NJ 930631). Proceed SW by A 98, passing the track to the remains of the Auchnagorth stone circle at NJ 839562. A diversion down the B 9027 to New Byth permits a view of this planned weavers' village of 1764. Return to the A 98 and in c 10 km note the long cairn of Longmanhill to the SW of a sharp bend (NJ 737620). Return to Banff via Macduff.

Buchan

The neolithic long cairn of Cairn Catto (no. 103) lies in a field to the W of a back road linking the A 952 Ellon/Peterhead and the A 950 Peterhead/New Pitsligo roads. After visiting the cairn, proceed N to the A 950 and turn left (W) for Longside village and church (no. 36). Carry on westwards through Mintlaw to Aden Country Park (no. 4), from which visitors may walk to Old Deer to see the old kirkyard and St Drostan's Episcopal church (with fine stained glass).

On returning to the A 950, turn left (W) for the Abbey of Deer (in 1.5 km at NJ 968481; limited opening hours: behind a high wall to the south of the road). Two km further W on the A 950, turn right (N) on a side road to Strichen to visit the Loudon Wood recumbent stone circle (no. 96) in the wood to the right (E) of the road. Just before entering Strichen turn left on the A 981 to visit the recumbent stone circle

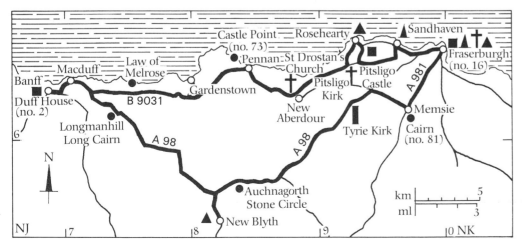

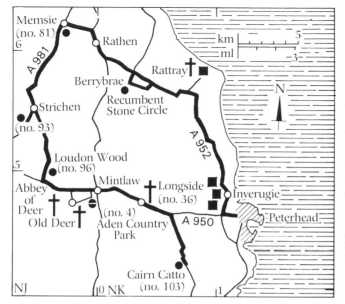

(no. 93) on the hill to the W which has been well restored. Pass through the substantial planned village of Strichen on the A 981 for Fraserburgh and in 7 km turn right (E) on B 9032 for the Memsie cairn (no. 81).

Proceed E and S through Rathen (on A 92 and A 952) and by a side road to pass the Berrybrae recumbent stone circle in trees in a field at NK 027571. Return to the A 952 and c 1 kms of Crimond turn left for the site of the medieval burgh of Rattray, at which the ruined Chapel of St Mary's and the castle mound can still be seen (NK 085575 and 087579). Travel S on the A 952 and turn off right past the prominent motte at NK 102486 for the remains of the castles of Inverugie (NK 102483) and Ravenscraig (NK 095487). Return to main road and enter Peterhead to visit the Museum (St Peter's Street) and the fine Square and Harbour.

Huntly Castle (no. 27): the
'airy sweetness of its oriels.'

BIBLIOGRAPHY

Aberdeen Civic Society   *Archibald Simpson Architect of Aberdeen 1790-1847*, Aberdeen, 1978.

Alexander, W   *Northern Rural Life*, 1870, reprinted Finzean, 1980.

Allan, JR   *North-East lowlands of Scotland*, London, 1952.

Burl, HAW   *The stone circles of the British Isles*, Yale, 1976.

Clarke, DV, Cowie, TG and Foxon, A   *Symbols of Power at the time of Stonehenge*, Edinburgh, 1985.

Close-Brooks, J and Stevenson, RBK   *Dark Age Sculpture*, Edinburgh, 1982.

Cruden, S   *The Scottish Castle*, Edinburgh, 1960; third edition, 1981.

Dunbar, JG   *The historic architecture of Scotland*, London, 1966; revised edition, 1978.

Fawcett, R   *Scottish medieval churches*, Edinburgh, 1985.

Fenton, A and Walker, B   *The rural architecture of Scotland*, Edinburgh, 1981.

Hamilton, R   *The Pluscarden Story*, Pluscarden, 1977.

Henshall, AS   *The chambered tombs of Scotland*, vols 1 & 2, Edinburgh, 1963 & 1972.

Howat, AJ and Seton, M   *Churches of Moray*, Elgin, 1981.

Hume, JR   *The industrial archaeology of Scotland*, II, *The Highlands and Islands*, London, 1977.

MacGibbon, D and Ross, T   *The Castellated and Domestic Architecture of Scotland*, Edinburgh, 5 vols, 1887-92.

Mellor, R and Smith, JS   *A visitors guide to Aberdeen*, Aberdeen, 1986.

Munro, RW   *Scottish Lighthouses*, Stornoway, 1979.

Murray, JC (ed)   *Excavations in the medieval burgh of Aberdeen*, 1973-81, Edinburgh, 1982.

Ogston, A   *The prehistoric antiquities of the Howe of Cromar*, Aberdeen, 1931.

Omand, D (ed)   *The Moray Book*, Edinburgh, 1976.

Omand, D (ed)   *The Grampian Book*, Golspie, 1986.

Ralston, I and Inglis, J   *Foul Hordes: the Picts in the North-East and their background*, Aberdeen, 1984.

Ralston, I, Sabine, K and Watt, W   'Later prehistoric settlements in north-east Scotland: a preliminary assessment', *in* Chapman, JC and Mytum, HC (eds), *Settlements in North Britain, 1000 BC–1000 AD*, Oxford, 149-73 (1983).

Royal Commission on the Ancient and Historical Monuments of Scotland, Archaeological Sites and Monuments Series, nos 15 (*South Kincardine*) and 21 (*North Kincardine*), Edinburgh, 1982 and 1984.

Ritchie, G and Ritchie, A   *Scotland: archaeology and early history*, London, 1981.

Scott, S   *The Castles of Mar*, Edinburgh, 1977.

Shepherd, IAG   *Powerful Pots: Beakers in north-east prehistory*, Aberdeen, 1986.

Shepherd, IAG and Ralston, IBM   *Early Grampian: a guide to the archaeology*, Aberdeen, 1979.

Simpson, WD   *The Province of Mar*, Aberdeen, 1944.

Simpson, WD   *The Earldom of Mar*, Aberdeen, 1949.

Skinner, BC   *Pluscarden Abbey*, Pluscarden, 1981.

Slade, HG   'Castle Fraser: a seat of the antient family of Fraser', *Proc Soc Antiq Scot*, 109 (1977-8), 233-300.

Smith, JS (ed)   *New light on medieval Aberdeen*, Aberdeen, 1985.

Tabraham, C   *Scottish castles and fortifications*, Edinburgh, 1986.

Tranter, N   *The Queen's Scotland. The eastern counties, Aberdeenshire, Angus and Kincardine*, London, 1972.

Tranter, N   *The Queen's Scotland. The north-east, the shires of Banff, Moray, Nairn , with Easter Inverness and Easter Ross*, London, 1974.

Watson, WH   *A. Marshall Mackenzie Architect in Aberdeen*, Aberdeen, 1985.

Wood, S   *The shaping of 19th-century Aberdeenshire*, Stevenage, 1985.

There are also well illustrated guide books to properties in the care of the National Trust for Scotland (Brodie Castle, Castle Fraser, Craigievar Castle, Crathes Castle, Drum Castle, Fyvie Castle, Haddo House and Leith Hall) and guide booklets or leaflets to those cared for by the Secretary of State for Scotland (Historic Buildings and Monuments: Balvenie Castle, Duff House, Elgin Cathedral, Kildrummy and Glenbuchat Castles, Tolquhon Castle, the Burghead Well, Corgarff Castle and Deer Abbey).

INDEX